Diane Carrington and Helen W...

Future Directions

Practical ways to develop
emotional intelligence
and **confidence** in
young people

Published by Network Educational Press Ltd
PO Box 635
Stafford
ST16 1BF

© Diane Carrington and Helen Whitten 2005

ISBN-13: 978 1 85539 198 7
ISBN-10   1 85539 198 8

Managing editor: Ann Baggaley
Design and layout: Peter Bailey for Proof Books
Cover design: Peter Bailey
Cartoons: Martin Aston at Just For Laffs
Proofreader: Lynn Bresler

Printed in Great Britain by Ashford Colour Press Ltd,
Gosport, Hants.

Pages marked with the symbol
may be photocopied for use in the purchasing institution

The diagrams and illustrations listed below are
available in full colour on the publisher's website
for use with the appropriate exercises. Go to
http://www.networkpress.co.uk/resources/
and click on the *Future Directions* link.

Handout 1:1, Thinking preferences; page 27,
Thinking process: wiring the brain; handout 5:1,
Thoughts impact emotions; handout 6:1,
Pressure points: causes of stress; handout 6:2:1,
The physiology of stress; handout 6:2:2,
Behavioural symptoms of stress; handout 9:3,
Mental video visualizing success; handout 12:2,
Detailed photo reading; handout 13:2, Your
elevator speech; handout 16:1, Word association
exercise; handout 19:3, Change success.

Acknowledgements
For their patience and encouragement, Diane
Carrington wishes to thank George, Sam, Nathan,
Hannah and her mother, while Helen Whitten wishes
to thank Rupert and Oliver. The authors are also
grateful to Langley Park School for Girls, Beckenham,
Kent, whose pupils trialled many of the exercises in
this book.

Shirley Conran OBE and The Work-Life Balance
Trust, and Caroline Waters of BT for their support.

The Thinking Preference diagram used in Exercise 1:1
is based on the Herrmann Brain Dominance
Instrument, developed by Ned Herrmann.

The principles written for a children's home in
Dharamsala, quoted on page 19, are taken from *For
Tibet with Love: A Beginner's Guide to Changing the
World* by Isabel Losada and are reprinted with kind
permission of Bloomsbury Publishing.

The quotation on the 'Inner Game', which appears on
page 38, is taken from *The Inner Game of Golf* by
Timothy Gallwey, published by Random House, Inc.,
New York.

The problem-solving technique in Exercise 8:2
(Basadur's Applied Creativity) is used with kind
permission of Dr Min Basadur.

Photographs, handout 13:1: Alamy Ltd

Mind Mapping® is the invention of Tony Buzan.

Contents

About the authors

Diane Carrington designs and delivers bespoke training sessions and workshops to a range of educational and business organizations throughout the world. She specializes in helping people to become more creative and to achieve their full potential in all situations in life and in work. She has worked with a range of organisations and with individuals of all ages.

Diane taught for eight years, as a Head of Department and a Head of Careers before returning to training and coaching ten years ago. She is keen to integrate the techniques and strategies that she uses successfully with adults into her work with young people. She works with Head Teachers, teachers and students and a range of educational organisations including the Learning and Skills Development Agency, the Learning Skills Council and the Confederation for British Teachers. She has also worked with the charity Parentline, training facilitators to enable them to deliver Parenting Skills courses.

Diane is currently studying for a Masters degree in Applied Psychology at Brunel University. She recently worked for the Samaritans on their Emotional Health and Well Being Project; designing and evaluating lesson plans for use by both teachers and Samaritan volunteers.

Helen Whitten has spent the last 13 years coaching and training young people and adults in practical methods for developing self-knowledge, self-confidence and the ability to maximize their potential. She has worked in organizations, schools and colleges teaching people how to train their minds to think positively and creatively about the situations they face. Helen applies cognitive-behavioural methodology to produce practical thinking strategies that enable people to break through old patterns of behaviour and develop emotions and behaviours that support their endeavours and ambitions. The result is an enthusiastic and optimistic attitude, clear goals consistent with personal values, practical skills and knowledge, and the ability to maintain performance under pressure.

Helen has applied these methods in her own life when she made a career change from work as a historical researcher to studying history as a mature student and retraining in the area of Human Resources and personal development. She founded Positiveworks in 1993 and has run individual and group sessions for clients throughout the world. Her first book *Your Mind at Work: Developing Self-Knowledge for Business Success*, is published by Kogan Page. She has also written *Age Matters: Employing, Managing and Motivating the Older Workforce* with Keren Smedley, to be published by Gower. Helen has produced CD-ROMs on *Help Yourself to a Better Life* and *How to Survive Life Positively*.

Helen and Diane work together in **Positiveworks Limited** offering coaching and training sessions on positive life strategies to young people and adults. These sessions include study skills, sixth-form induction programmes, sessions to prepare for interviews and sessions based on the exercises included in this book. They speak at educational conferences and deliver staff training. For further information visit www.positiveworks.com.

Introducing the book

Aim

The aim of this book is to support you in giving young people skills and strategies to develop emotional well-being and an understanding of the behaviours required to manage adult life. It is now recognized that emotional intelligence is a key ingredient for success in academic achievement, social relationships and career development. Whether you are a teacher, parent, career adviser, mentor or social worker we believe that anyone working with young people will find this book helpful, and where the book sometimes refers to teachers, this should be taken as meaning all those involved in guiding young people. Government initiatives are highlighting the benefits of emotional health and well-being in reducing truancy and increasing motivation within schools, and these topics are included within the school curriculum areas of PSHE, citizenship and career guidance, as well as permeating many other subject areas. This book supports these initiatives, and more.

We have been practising as personal development trainers and coaches, with a background in teaching, for 20 years. A frequent comment from our adult participants is *'we needed these skills when we were at school and when we started work!'*. After subsequent research with young people we found similar concerns such as:

Why do I always seem to say the wrong thing?
I don't know how to tell my teachers how I really feel.
I am frightened of making the wrong decision about my future.
I don't know how I am supposed to cope with exams, coursework and my Saturday job.
Nothing prepared me for my first week at work.
I didn't understand what was expected of me.
How do I communicate with difficult adults?
I wish I'd sought more advice about my job options.
I messed up my job interviews because I didn't know how to manage stress.

The topic areas of this book are designed to give you theoretical and practical models that can be easily adapted to the precise needs, concerns and goals of young people of all ability levels. We have trialled all these exercises with a range of ages and abilities, from disaffected young people to high-achieving school-leavers and undergraduates.

The sessions have ranged from one-off 40-minute lessons to a six-week course of two hours per week. The exercises have been undertaken individually, in class-size groups, peer-group settings, family environments, and in sessions with a specific focus such as developing confidence for interviews. Comments have included:

I realized that if I want something in life I have to go and do it.
I now feel more confident and prepared.
I understand better where I am coming from.
I didn't realize other people felt like this.
I now know what I can do next time I get really cross!

All of these sessions have been enthusiastically received. Many of the behaviours and techniques have been successfully adopted by the young participants and the sessions have also provided a safe forum for the discussion of sensitive issues. Students, teachers, facilitators, parents and mentors have commented that these discussions could be challenging but were also valuable and insightful and helped to build a greater understanding of the pressures on young people today.

The numerous opportunities available to young people in today's world can be overwhelming. This book aims to equip them with the skills to feel confident, manage difficult emotions and take responsibility for their lives at this stage. This will help them make a successful transition from education to the workplace and to feel confident in the choices they make about the future. The tools and techniques that we have devised will provide you with challenging interactive materials to engage students and help them to focus on the future, in this uncertain period of their lives.

The whole purpose of this programme is to empower the young people with whom you are working to:

- develop self-knowledge;
- manage emotions and build positive relationships;
- feel confident as they enter the adult world;
- reflect on the consequences of their behaviours;
- make informed choices about college and career;
- take responsibility for their future.

How to use this book

This book is a resource for you to use. Each chapter contains a specific topic area that can be delivered as a stand-alone session, or as part of a modular programme. The topics follow a logical process, designed to be undertaken in a chronological order if possible. Section 1, *Emotional well-being*, is the foundation stone of the programme. It provides the theoretical basis that underpins the whole book and gives students essential lifeskills. The last chapter requires the students to review the whole programme and plan how they will use the learning in the future.

Each chapter will provide you with all the information you require for one session, with resources and handouts that can be photocopied and given to the student. We offer a range of exercises and although we have focused on class-sessions you can choose which are relevant and adapt the book to your needs. It is recommended that the student files the handouts and any notes they make so that they can refer to them in the future.

For rapid identification, all handout pages display the symbol

For easy reference, each chapter follows the same template:

1 Definition of the subject.
2 Benefits of the subject.
3 Experts' opinions.
4 A story to share.
5 Three interactive exercises from which you can choose to do one, two or all three in a session, a class or as homework. These can be undertaken individually or in groups.
6 Discussion points for a plenary.
7 Six Tips and handout information relating to the subject.

Method of delivery

The purpose of this programme is to give young people a confident start in life, and self-belief. Some individuals may have previously underperformed in academic subjects but this material deals with another aspect of their potential – their ability to become emotionally intelligent. This has been proven to be a key ingredient for success in life. They may therefore need to be given a fresh start, as your support and belief in them is an essential component of their future success. Often we have found that an element of self-disclosure alters the usual adult–student relationship and encourages trust.

In these sessions it is hoped that the adult will be able to adopt a 'coaching' style in order to draw out answers from the students rather than provide them with solutions. Through a series of questions, each interactive exercise is designed to enable the students to stop and think and identify what they really feel and want for themselves outside other influences. Therefore a safe and supportive environment is required to establish an open and honest forum where young people feel they can share without judgement.

To achieve this, it would be advantageous to agree a list of ground rules with the student, whether you are working individually or in a group. Ground rules agreeing how you wish to work together will help them feel comfortable and at the same time give them responsibility for their behaviour and contribution. After a brief discussion, these rules could be recorded and, if possible, displayed on a sheet of paper, flip chart or whiteboard and brought out at subsequent sessions. If *honesty, listening to each other, not putting other people down, respect, confidentiality, contributing* or *open-mindedness* do not come from the students you might wish to suggest them yourself. In this way you have an agreed contract, which can be referred back to if this behaviour is not practised.

Some of the exercises are designed to be done in small peer groups, but if you are working individually, for example, parent–child or career advisor–student, you have the option either to ask them to bring a friend or classmate, or for you, as facilitator, to participate in the exercise yourself (for example, Exercise 7:1:1). In doing so, you can participate in a discussion on the topic, while encouraging the young person to think about it and share thoughts and ideas. Similarly, in Exercise 7:3 HELPful coaching, it would be best if possible for the teacher/mentor to include another person in the session but if this is not feasible, you should choose a topic and become the 'coachee' yourself in order to help the student practise coaching skills. Exercise 11:3 is another instance where, if you are working individually, you can join the debate yourself as teacher/adult. In a family group or peer group session, there should be one adult who does not participate in the debate but who remains as objective facilitator.

Potentially sensitive issues

As the interactive exercises will inevitably involve students exploring and analysing themselves, their hopes and their fears, the topics may touch on some sensitive issues. For this reason we have included details of supporting organizations and useful contacts in *Resources* on page 191, which could be displayed at the beginning of each session. This alerts students to the fact that there is support outside the classroom on specific issues and does not require them to have to ask for information, which may embarrass them. In some schools and colleges it might be possible to give the name of a person with whom issues can be discussed in depth if required.

If these sessions are conducted in a home environment it might be useful to encourage the young person to seek further information from specific organisations such as those listed in the *Resources* section.

Plenary session

Each lesson or session plan finishes with a plenary. The plenaries are an important time for the facilitator to pull together the main messages and learning points of the exercise. It is also a way of helping the young person to share feelings and experiences and raise any topics they have opinions or concerns about. In this way the adult can become aware of any further support that the student may need.

Section 1
Emotional well-being

1 Developing self-knowledge

At bottom, every man knows well enough that he is a unique human being,
only once on this earth; and by no extraordinary chance will such a marvellously
picturesque piece of diversity in unity as he is, ever be put together a second time.
FRIEDRICH WILHELM NIETZSCHE (1844–1900)

SELF-KNOWLEDGE is crucial if young people are going to make good decisions about their futures. As they move from education into the workplace it is helpful if they are aware of their own identities and goals beyond the expectations of parents and teachers. This helps them to be true to themselves. It is also important that students recognize their strengths and talents so as to be able to communicate them to others at interviews, college and at work. Knowing their weaknesses identifies areas for development and gives them an understanding of how their behaviour and communication style impact on others.

This chapter will help you enable young people to recognize their unique strengths and personal qualities so as to build confidence and self-esteem. It is proven by modern genetics that there is no person in the world who is exactly the same as another – nor has there ever been one in the past, nor will there ever be one in the future. Helping young people appreciate this allows them to make their unique contribution in all environments, capitalizing on strengths, to have a positive impact and influence on others. Most of all, self-knowledge also builds confidence and emotional maturity.

The benefits of self-knowledge

There are some important moments in their lives when self-knowledge helps students to make decisions, make an impression and to build relationships. If they don't know who they are they cannot put themselves across to others to advantage. These key moments include:

- meeting someone for the first time;
- understanding the impact they have on others;
- going for a university or job interview;
- taking exams;
- taking oral exams;
- first day at work;
- first date;
- making decisions about college or career;
- recognizing personal strengths and weaknesses.

What the experts say

'Know thyself' has been a statement used by philosophers, psychologists and religious leaders for centuries. Without stopping to think who you are you can go down the wrong path and make life choices that do not reflect who you are but reflect the needs and influences of those around you. Shakespeare wrote 'To thine own self be true' – but if we do not know who the self is we cannot be true to ourselves.

Discussing nature versus nurture, the geneticist Steven Pinker (2002) writes in *The Blank Slate* that genetics are a strong determiner of a person's results but that the awareness of family patterns can enable people to break out of them and achieve what they want for themselves.

A story to share

Tony's parents wanted him to be an accountant. In his heart he didn't really feel this was the right job for him but he wasn't sure that he could succeed in the arts – which was where he felt more 'at home' – and so he allowed himself to be persuaded to do what they wanted.

Two years into his training, Tony decided he could no longer bear to undertake a career that he did not feel reflected who he was. Much to his parents' anguish and confusion, he decided to leave accountancy and retrain as a picture framer. After a few years he set up his own art gallery and picture-framing business. Tony's self-belief increased, he married an artist and has been running a successful business ever since.

Three steps to knowing yourself

You can choose whether to do all the following exercises or just use one or two that you feel are the most relevant to the students. Each of the three exercises can either build on one another or stand alone.

Exercise 1:1 Building self-knowledge

In order to develop self-appreciation young people need to reflect on their own strengths and successes, big or small. In this exercise they can think back over their whole lifetime and record their successes. Encourage them not to be modest. Explain that if they do not recognize their own successes and strengths they will not be able to explain them to others. Warn them that their negative 'thinking' voice may try to convince them they have nothing to write – tell them not to listen!

Aim To help students recognize their strengths and personal qualities. Very often young people are given more criticism than praise.

Benefit Recognizing their own strengths means that they will be able to express them at interviews and in the workplace.

Materials required:
- Photocopies of handout 1:1 (see *www.networkpress.co.uk/resources* for colour version) and Six Tips for each individual
- Flip chart, whiteboard or paper to record ideas and actions

Session plan
1 Introduce the concepts of self-knowledge and self-awareness.
2 Ask the students to share some situations where they will need these.
3 Ask them to consider the benefits of being able to identify and explain their strengths, personal qualities and talents.
4 Give them the handouts and allow 10–15 minutes for completing the Thinking Preferences questionnaire. Tell them to focus only on the positive.
5 Put them in twos or threes and suggest they share their strengths and interests with others. Help them to realize that modesty is not appropriate here.
6 Plenary:
    - What has been learned?
    - How might they build on this exercise?
    - When might the skill of self-knowledge be useful?

Thinking preferences

People develop habits and preferences with regard to what they like to think about. Four thinking styles are depicted in the diagram below. The upper (theoretical) left 'A' mode of thinking can be described as analytical, mathematical, technical and problem solving. The lower (practical) left 'B' mode can be described as controlled, conservative, planned, organized and administrative in nature. The lower (feeling) right 'C' mode is interpersonal, emotional, musical, spiritual and 'talking', and the upper (ideas/experimental) right 'D' mode is imaginative, synthesizing, artistic, holistic and conceptual. The figure below is based on the Herrmann Brain Dominance Instrument. This measures activity across the complex nerve pathways that flow between the left and right cortices (outer layers) of the brain.

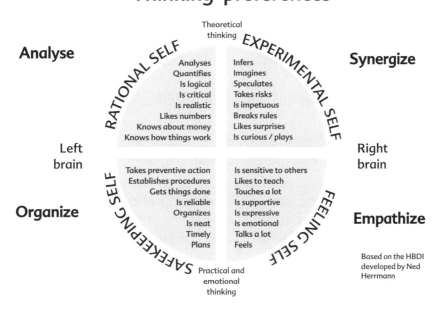

Thinking preferences

Based on the HBDI developed by Ned Herrmann

Thinking preferences questionnaire

Look at the lists of words below and circle the SUBJECTS that most interest you, with 1 being least preferred and 5 being most preferred. Total each list and see which quadrant you prefer.

A MODE

Mathematical	1	2	3	4	5
Technical	1	2	3	4	5
Financial	1	2	3	4	5
Detailed	1	2	3	4	5
Rational	1	2	3	4	5
Critical	1	2	3	4	5
Analytical	1	2	3	4	5
Engineering	1	2	3	4	5
Sciences	1	2	3	4	5

B MODE

Procedures	1	2	3	4	5
Administration	1	2	3	4	5
Organizing	1	2	3	4	5
Writing	1	2	3	4	5
Projects	1	2	3	4	5
Quality standards	1	2	3	4	5
Visible results	1	2	3	4	5
Systems	1	2	3	4	5
Planning	1	2	3	4	5

D MODE

Big picture	1	2	3	4	5
New ideas	1	2	3	4	5
Innovation	1	2	3	4	5
Entrepreneurial	1	2	3	4	5
Creative	1	2	3	4	5
Sales	1	2	3	4	5
Breaking rules	1	2	3	4	5
Future-oriented	1	2	3	4	5
Design	1	2	3	4	5

C MODE

Communicating	1	2	3	4	5
Teambuilding	1	2	3	4	5
Expressing	1	2	3	4	5
Teaching	1	2	3	4	5
Mentoring	1	2	3	4	5
Encouraging	1	2	3	4	5
Cooperating	1	2	3	4	5
Feeling	1	2	3	4	5
Caring	1	2	3	4	5

Exercise 1:2 Achievements

This exercise introduces the pupils to Mind Mapping®, a thinking tool invented by Tony Buzan that provides a way of recording ideas and information in a memorable, graphic way. Your students may well be familiar with this technique and the exercise gives them the opportunity to practise.

Aim To get students into the habit of noticing their achievements, small and large, on a regular basis.

Benefit Being able to identify and appreciate personal achievements builds confidence and will enable the students to feel proud of their successes.

Materials required:
- Photocopies of handout 1:2 and Six Tips for each individual
- Flip chart, whiteboard or paper to record ideas and actions

Session plan
1 Introduce the subject of 'achievements' to the group. You can start by asking them whose achievements they admire and why – for example, a sportsperson, a politician, writer, singer and so on.
2 Lead the conversation to more personal examples – a parent, aunt, uncle, brother or sister.
3 Now give them the handout and ask them to complete this by adding personal achievements onto each line of the Mind Map®. Allow them five to ten minutes.
4 When they have finished ask them to stand up and take their Achievement maps and walk around the room looking at each other's maps and achievements. Help them to develop the ability to congratulate one another – many children enjoy putting others down. Help them to appreciate their own and their peer group's achievements.
5 Plenary:
   - What have they noticed about one another?
   - How did it feel to share achievements?
   - Has it given them any ideas about what they might like to develop?
   - How might they find sharing achievements useful?

Achievements map

Focus on specific achievements. Write down as many as possible, one on each line — add more lines if necessary. These can be anything that you consider to be an achievement — for example, getting homework in on time; finding your way across a new town to see a friend; passing an exam; helping a friend with a project; arranging your gap year travel; passing your driving test; a holiday job; producing a painting.

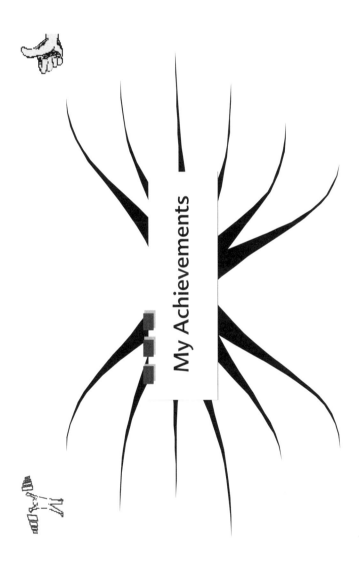

Exercise 1:3 Best-self visualization

This asks young people to identify what they feel like when they feel at their best. They can write their ideas up on a flip chart or whiteboard, or share them on paper. Explain that they can re-create this feeling any time they want. Lead them through it – ask them to stand up and show you what they look like when they are at their best. For example, standing taller, more energized, smiling, confident.

Aim To help students identify the ingredients of their uniqueness and character.

Benefit To value themselves, be able to describe their strengths and develop their weaknesses and develop self-acceptance and self-appreciation.

Materials required:
- Photocopy of Six Tips for each individual
- Paper and pens
- Flip chart, whiteboard or paper to record ideas and actions
- Cut-outs of photographs of politicians and celebrities looking 'at their best' and 'at their worst'

Session plan
1 Explain that everyone in this world has strengths and weaknesses – you can be president of the United States, chief executive of a major company, a pop idol or celebrity but still have areas of vulnerability alongside the strengths and talents.
2 Ask them to imagine that they were going to make a movie about themselves feeling at their best and about their lives so far. Help them to identify how they would set this up; how they would describe themselves; what the script story might be; and how this character might interact with others.
3 Give them some time to write a short brief for the film director incorporating these factors.
4 Put the students in twos and give each person three minutes to describe what he or she has written, without interruption.
5 They can then have time to share feelings and offer supportive ideas and feedback.
6 Plenary:
   - What might it feel like to be the star of a movie?
   - Did this exercise give them any more insights into themselves and their characters/behaviour?

Developing self-knowledge

Six Tips

1 Start a journal and record what works in your life.

2 Note down positive comments that other people say about you.

3 Focus on the positive aspects of your life and your achievements.

4 Learn from the things that go wrong but don't become a victim to events.

5 Observe yourself from time to time as if you were a film director and notice what you see and how to develop your strengths.

6 Remember that no one has exactly the same thoughts and ideas, so share yours, listen to others and express yourself in groups.

Why bother?

- We now live in a global environment. Wherever you live there is competition from other nationalities for university places and jobs. You are not always encouraged to express your strengths and talents. It is necessary that you start to do so because many other cultures are more forthright about demonstrating their successes and achievements. This does not mean boasting or being arrogant but it does mean that you need to value what you have created and experienced.

- Life can change in an instant. The company you work for might be taken over or someone might enter your department who is better at putting across his or her strengths than you are. Realize that you are being observed, so demonstrate your skills daily – don't get complacent. Equally, remember that you can choose to transfer these skills into another company.

- When you value and appreciate yourself this helps others to value and appreciate you.

My first action step

Commit yourself to one action step over the next week that will help you to develop self-knowledge.

This week I shall:

....

....

....

....

....

....

....

Future Directions © Diane Carrington and Helen Whitten (Network Educational Press, 2005)

2 Identifying personal values

This above all: to thine own self be true... [Hamlet]
WILLIAM SHAKESPEARE (1564–1616)

If you tell the truth you don't have to remember anything.
MARK TWAIN (1835–1910)

VALUES GUIDE good decisions and 'right' action. It is therefore helpful for students to initiate the process of identifying their personal values at as early a stage as possible in their lifetimes. Without values a person can be led astray into actions that may not reflect the person he or she really feels he or she is or wants to be. This can relate to disruptive behaviour in the playground, to being influenced into taking drugs or having sex with someone when he or she doesn't really want to, or to unethical behaviour in the boardroom. Just as small children can be influenced to do something naughty against their will, or teenagers influenced to take an academic subject that their parents and not themselves feel is best for them, so adults can equally be drawn into the wrong careers or, worse, into fraud, dishonesty or deceit by a strong character who may not understand their values nor have their best interests at heart. Learning to identify and express personal values is therefore crucial to effective relationship building.

This chapter is designed to help students consider and identify their personal values and be able to express them to others. It can be helpful to explain that these values may change as they go through life (though they often don't) but that they will provide them with a compass for good decisions when faced with options of behaviour or action.

The benefits of identifying personal values

Feeling confident about their personal values and staying true to themselves can help young people in many important aspects of life, including

- choosing friends;
- planning an academic course that reflects what they care about;
- standing up to people who try to persuade them to do things they do not really want to do;
- making a career choice;
- making decisions;
- resolving conflicting priorities;
- self-expression.

What the experts say

In Stephen Covey's book *The Seven Habits of Highly Effective People* (1989) he cites the importance of strong values and principles as the guide for happiness, success and peace of mind. One has only to see the newspaper articles relating the spectacular fall of certain corporate bodies and the individuals within them to realize that forfeiting values can bring a person's downfall. One wrong decision – whether to lie or cheat – can sometimes ruin a life. All philosophies and religions give guidelines for living a good life, and none pretends it is easy, but living and working in a way that is aligned to personal values tends to raise self-esteem and bring a sense of personal success.

An example of value-based behaviours can be seen in the Principles written in a children's home in Dharamsala, the town where the Dalai Lama resides:

- Look for the good in a person if you feel like saying something mean.
- Apologizing doesn't always mean you were in the wrong – it means you are sorry.
- When someone has been successful, compliment them.
- Try to make others feel better when they make mistakes.
- Let your friends have other friends.

Living by values is an everyday consideration – from how children talk to parents or siblings as they leave home in the mornings, to their behaviour at school or college, to the major life decisions they will take.

A story to share

Mary went away to university some distance from her home. One good schoolfriend, Jo, went to the same university and Mary was very happy to have her companionship during freshers' week. However, she soon came to realize that her new group of university friends did not like Jo and that she risked being alienated if she continued to be friends with her. Mary felt nervous of losing the approval of the group and broke off her friendship with Jo in order to be part of this new clique. Had Mary listed 'loyalty' as one of her values she might have remained friends with Jo and taken the risk that this might isolate her from one group of friends; eventually she may have benefited by drawing to her a set of friends who also found loyalty important.

Three steps to identifying personal values

These exercises are designed to help students consider what values are, identify their own values and understand how to apply them.

Exercise 2:1 What do you value?

Some young people can find it difficult to be specific about what things really matter to them. In this exercise you can help them by thinking first of objects that they value, which are often easier to identify than concepts or feelings. This can be particularly true of young people who have experienced learning difficulties or other disadvantages. However, it is important to help them to understand that their personal qualities, family, friends, pets, and being able to feel proud of themselves and their behaviour, are ultimately what matter most.

Aim To enable the students to identify and appreciate what is important in their lives.

Benefit Identifying what objects they value can demonstrate some aspect of themselves and what they might value in themselves and others. This has nothing to do with wealth, as many objects that people value are things such as photographs, or comfort items and memorabilia.

Materials required:
- Photocopy of Six Tips for each individual
- Plain paper and pens

Session plan

1 Introduce the concept of values and explain how successful people and leaders have emphasized and relied upon the importance of strong values to help them make good decisions and lead lives they feel proud of. Help them realize this is not just for leaders nor just for 'special occasions' but for every day.

2 Have a general discussion about what the students value.

3 To help them be more specific, ask them to imagine a scenario where a house is on fire and they have the opportunity to rescue just two items.

4 Give them a few minutes to think about this and write down (a) what they would rescue; (b) the reasons for doing so.

5 Plenary:
   - Compare the suggestions.
   - Are there any similarities?
   - Is it possible to put the items into categories?
   - What is the most popular type of item?
   - What does this tell us about what we value?
   - How does valuing objects compare to valuing people?
   - Can they think of the people they value most?
   - In what ways can they value their own inner strengths?

Exercise 2:2 Value list

Students will see a list of values options and will need to consider which of these are important to them personally. They will then be asked to rank these values in order of highest priority so as to focus their minds on the things they personally care about.

Aim To help students identify their personal values.

Benefit To start the process of understanding the concept of values and also the part values can play in life's decisions and actions.

Materials required:
- Photocopies of handout 2:2 and Six Tips for each individual
- Flip chart, whiteboard or paper to record comments

Session plan
1 Introduce the concept of values.
2 Ask the students to share some of their personal ideas about values and some examples of where they may have witnessed values in action, either in their personal lives or in the media (for example, stories of politicians who are not 'walking their talk').
3 Give them the values list and give them a period of time to read through it.
4 Ask them to list their ten priority values and, if possible, to rank them in order.
5 Suggest that they write their ten values on a flip chart or piece of paper.
6 Plenary:
   - Do they have the same values as their friends?
   - Can they give examples of when they have made decisions or taken actions according to these values?
   - Can they think of a time when they stood apart from their friends and stood by their personal values rather than the values of a group?
   - How might they continue to apply these values in their daily lives?

What I value in life

Study this list and tick the options you feel are important to you. Copy the ten that you consider the most important to you into the box below. There are no wrong or right answers!

Security	Friendship
Change	Challenge
Travel	Status
Caring for others	Personal growth
Charity	Adventure
Creativity	World peace
Harmony	Spirituality
Contribution	Making a difference
The environment	Peace of mind
Generating wealth for others	Wealth
Writing	Co-operation
The quiet life	Power
Health	Happiness
Ideas	Integrity
Music	Recognition
Invention and innovation	Patriotism
Expertise	Respect
General knowledge	Loyalty
Tolerance	Independence
Compassion	Wisdom
Altruism	Teamwork
Eccentricity	Leisure
Conformity	Variety
Family	Achievement

List the ten values you consider most important to you in the right-hand column:

1 ....
2 ....
3 ....
4 ....
5 ....
6 ....
7 ....
8 ....
9 ....
10 ....

Exercise 2:3 What is success?

In this exercise, individuals are asked to consider whether being in a certain career makes a person successful or whether it is the calibre and behaviour of the person that makes them successful.

Aim To help the young people identify what success means to them.

Benefit Helps the students to identify what they value in terms of career and style of person, and also helps them to choose and make decisions.

Materials required:
- Photocopies of handout 2:3 and Six Tips for each individual
- Flip chart, whiteboard or paper to record comments

Session plan
1 Discuss the concept of success further – is it related to what someone does? Is it position? Status? Money? Achievements?
2 Suggest they look at the handout and tick the careers they see as 'successful'.
3 Suggest they think of other careers to add to the list.
4 Plenary:
   - What did the students find?
   - What are their conclusions with regard to the perception of success?
   - Is it the role/career itself or the way a person behaves that makes them think of someone as successful?
   - Help them to understand that their values play a role in what they identify as success – for example, if money is a value they will possibly see celebrities, or bankers or lawyers, as successful. If altruism or contribution are their most important values they are more likely to see a nurse, doctor or social worker as successful.
   - What behaviours make them feel proud of themselves?
   - What tasks or actions make them feel good about themselves?

What is success?

Look at the page below to help you consider which careers and what type of person you see as successful. Tick those you think are successful, and write in any others as appropriate, giving reasons for your answers in the second column.

What or who is a success in your eyes? Tick those on the list below whom you admire. What attributes or qualities do you respect? Consider what attributes you would like to develop yourself.

Sports stars ❏	Politicians ❏	Actors ❏
Writers ❏	Statesmen ❏	Media ❏
Rebels ❏	Charity workers ❏	Inventors ❏
Business people ❏	Thinkers ❏	Architects ❏
Teachers ❏	Designers ❏	Film ❏
Nurses ❏	Entrepreneurs ❏	Engineers ❏
Doctors ❏	Celebrities ❏	Artists ❏
Scientists ❏	Pop & music ❏	IT/Technical ❏
Lawyers ❏	Classical musicians ❏	Social workers ❏
Bankers ❏	Armed Forces ❏	Police ❏

What other careers and options might you consider?

What are the reasons for your choices?

1 ....
2 ....
3 ....
4 ....
5 ....
6 ....
7 ....
8 ....
9 ....
10 ....

Future Directions © Diane Carrington and Helen Whitten (Network Educational Press, 2005)

Identifying personal values

Six Tips

1 Make decisions aligned to your values and not those of other people. It is easy to bend to pressure from your peers or from older people, but think carefully before taking action that does not conform to your own values.

2 Your values may change as you go through life. This may happen because of the particular stage of life you are in or it may happen through personal experiences. Be ready for this, take others' viewpoints into account but make decisions based on your personal values.

3 Value yourself, your uniqueness, your personal views and others will be more likely to respect you.

4 Don't measure yourself against others.

5 Each person has a right to their own values.

6 Consider your personal values when you are making choices about your career and the type of organization you want to work for.

Why bother?

■ Identifying and living by your personal values raises your self-esteem. When you take action that is not congruent with your values you can demean yourself and this increases your stress levels. Increased stress levels, as you will see in Chapter 6, deplete your immune system and put you at risk of illness.

■ In the twenty-first century, much comment has been made of the lack of 'trust' of government and corporate behaviours. These relate to personal values, as trust is built through 'walking your talk' – that is, living and acting in the way you talk. Therefore, if you want people to trust you, the more you are able to behave and act in a way that is congruent to your personal values the more you are likely to gain the trust of others.

My first action step

Commit yourself to one action step over the next week that will help you to live by your personal values.

This week I shall:

....

....

....

....

....

....

3 Mindpower: how the brain works

I have nothing to declare except my genius.
OSCAR WILDE (1854–1900)

I find that the harder I work, the more luck I seem to have.
THOMAS JEFFERSON (1743–1826)

The way people use their minds is the key to success. We have discovered a great deal about how the brain works over the last 10 to 20 years and this information can be applied to help people live and work at their optimum. This chapter covers three areas:

1 how the brain works
2 how to learn
3 how to change habits of thought and behaviour.

The benefits of knowing how the brain works

In every situation that the students find themselves in it will be beneficial if they manage to use their brains more efficiently. Such situations include:

- making the most of every day;
- managing new situations;
- studying and gaining qualifications;
- motivating yourself;
- working through problems and challenges;
- communicating;
- adapting;
- mind, health and energy.

What the experts say

Neuroscience has demonstrated that the brain evolves and changes shape every moment of our lives. We have approximately 100 billion neurons (nerve cells) and a trillion glial cells, which support and protect neurons. As we think, remember, learn and imagine, electrochemical messages are being sent from one brain cell to the next and this amazing network is capable of performing 20 million brain calculations per second.

Developing our neural pathways of thought gives us our unique personality and sense of identity. No two brains are alike. Although there are 'general areas' that can be located within each person's brain, the way a person has used his or her brain builds the connections and thus the shape of the brain on a second-by-second daily basis. For example, the brain of London cab drivers has a particularly large hippocampus region where spatial memory is stored. In certain types of brain surgery, a patient is kept awake, so that his or her responses allow the surgeon to pinpoint vital control areas without risk of damage.

The main message we can receive from neuroscience is that, although the brain may have some genetic predispositions, now that we understand how to build neural pathways it is possible to accept that every human being can develop potential. In today's world there are plenty of examples of people who did badly at school but who studied later in life – sometimes gaining an academic degree in their 70s or 80s. Others have developed business or artistic talents. A 63 year old who was an IBM executive has recently discovered a talent for portraiture.

Thinking process: wiring the brain

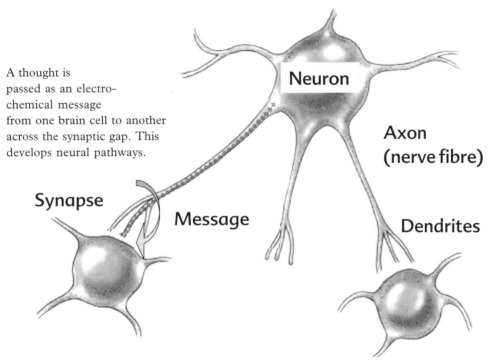

A thought is passed as an electro-chemical message from one brain cell to another across the synaptic gap. This develops neural pathways.

This diagram can be found in colour on the publisher's website, www.networkpress.co.uk/resources

By conscious learning and repetitive practice, we can develop new neural pathways of thought, learning and behaviour until the day we die. It is no longer relevant to say 'I am who I am' but more true to say: 'I am who I am today but I may be different tomorrow.'

Ned Herrmann was the founder of the concept of 'whole brain technology', which followed his research into thinking and the brain to understand and develop creativity within corporate teams. He developed and validated the Herrmann Brain Dominance Instrument, an assessment tool used by over a million people worldwide. Herrmann worked with Nobel Prize winner Professor Roger W. Sperry, who was responsible for developing some of the theories of the left and right brain functions based on his work with stroke patients. More recently, neuroscientists have come to understand that the left–right brain functions are far more complex than had originally been thought. However, the theory still has its uses as a simplified way of categorizing types of brain activity.

Left and right brain cortex functions

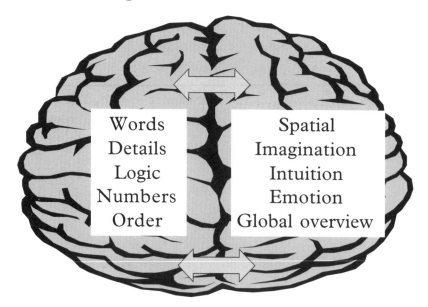

Words	Spatial
Details	Imagination
Logic	Intuition
Numbers	Emotion
Order	Global overview

Arrows show that messages pass between left and right cortices

A young person's brain has innate potential for development. Some individuals may be more competent in what are known as 'left-brain' activities, such as mathematics, language and analysis. These tend to be the areas that are valued in education and in much of the professional workplace. This can lead to big picture thinkers or creative/practical pupils feeling inadequate. The more inadequate they feel the less they achieve and it can become a downward spiral.

It is important to help all students to realize that they can always develop other areas of their brains and other areas of potential talent and strengths – by practice and repetition. All organizations and businesses require a combined mixture of skills. Facts and figures alone do not allow for the global context of a situation, or for innovation or customer focus. People of all types can find valuable and fulfilling work and can continue to develop new skills and strengths for the rest of their lives.

What people achieve is due to the focus of their minds and where they choose to place their energy and intentions. It may take years to reach a goal, but if it is something they really want then all the hard work is worthwhile. Persistence, dedication and self-belief are all keys to success.

Stories to share

- A boy who was bottom of the class had some coaching sessions, learned about how his brain and memory worked, how to mind map and get key points from his textbooks, and came top of his class within a term.
- Dominic O'Brien was bored at school and left when he was 16. He taught himself memory skills and became World Memory Champion!
- A 77 year old tripled his reading speed and gained a degree in Egyptology.
- A 43-year-old woman, who had concentrated on bringing up her children in her earlier years, took a degree, retrained and started a new and successful business.

Three steps to mindpower

The three exercises in this chapter are designed to help students understand how to maximize their ability to learn to learn. They will go through a strong learning curve when they enter college or the workplace and it will help them to feel really confident if they are able to read, remember and learn information effectively.

Exercise 3:1 Mapping thoughts to enhance memory

This exercise uses Mind Mapping®, which was introduced in Exercise 1:2. It also focuses on the students themselves so as to give them subject matter to develop in the map. You can always vary the topic and encourage them to use Mind Mapping® for other exercises, too.

Aim   To demonstrate that structuring thoughts, ideas and information in a visual graphic format, using a student's own logical associations and order, enhances learning and memory.

Benefit   Students often imagine that learning and study finish as they leave education but they need to learn new things for the rest of their lives. Feeling confident of the ability to learn to learn is therefore a key skill. It is possible to develop systems of thinking and working to achieve peak performance.

Materials required:
- Photocopies of handout 3:1 and Six Tips for each individual
- Plain white (unlined) paper
- Coloured pens or felt-tips
- Flip chart, whiteboard or lined paper

Session plan
1   Introduce the concept of visual mapping of information and explain that the benefits are greater comprehension, structure, analysis and recall.
2   Show them, by whatever means appropriate, how a Mind Map® builds up, using the handout as a template.
3   Suggest an easy topic – for example, 'Me and My Life' (see example).
4   Get the students to share the information on their maps with some other pupils.
5   Plenary:
   ■ Discuss how this went.
   ■ Encourage the use of mapping for essay plans, revision, problem solving, goal setting, interview plans and so on.

Making a map of your life

Below you will see a Mind Map® describing the main principles of Mind Mapping® as invented by Tony Buzan:

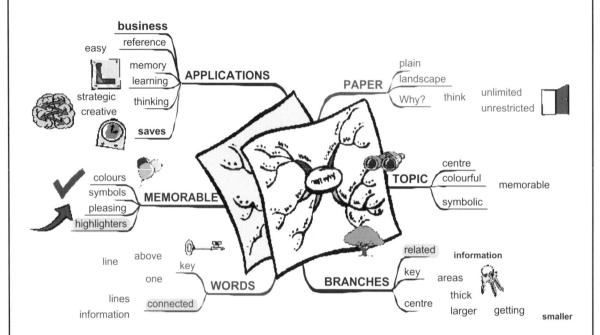

Map on MindManager software

How to map

Make your own map, using the 'Me' map shown here as a guide:

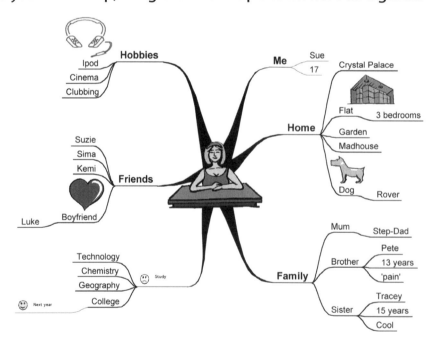

Map on MindManager software

- Take plain paper, landscape.
- Start with the topic in the middle of the page.
- Build branches of key related areas from there.

- Just use key words and images, on top of the line.
- Build information and ideas using personal associations.
- Use colour for better recall.

Future Directions © Diane Carrington and Helen Whitten (Network Educational Press, 2005)

Exercise 3:2 Learning to learn

This exercise is designed to help students think about how they learn best. They can also visit the Network Educational Press website to explore the Learning Style Analysis™. Knowing how they learn best can help students devise an environment and time-management system that best suits their personal learning style.

Aim To demonstrate the learning process and to help each student realize that we all learn in different ways.

Benefit By learning to learn, students can adapt study technique to preferred style and feel confident when entering college or the workplace, or changing to a new job, that they will be able to absorb new information effectively. Even knowing something as simple as the fact that an extrovert needs to express his or her ideas whereas an introvert is more likely to be content sitting in a library, can be helpful to the learning process.

Materials required:
- Photocopies of handout 3:2 and Six Tips for each individual
- Visit **http://www.networkpress.co.uk/lsa/** to learn about the Learning Style Analysis™ supplied by Network Educational Press

Session plan
1 Explain that learning is a mental, physical, emotional and sensory process.
2 Explain that all of us learn in different ways and many of these are sensory as the brain memorizes through seeing, hearing, doing, touching, tasting and feeling.
3 Learning review – give them the handout and ask them to complete it individually.
4 Put them in small groups to discuss their findings and to observe and discuss the differences.
5 Plenary:
   - Have they always found the same subjects interesting/easy throughout their school life?
   - Have they experienced finding a subject difficult and then breaking through to master it?
   - How can they apply this knowledge in the future, to continue to learn well?

Learning review

It is easy to assume that learning finishes when you leave school but you will continue to learn new things until the day you die. Every time you listen to the news, or if you go to college, start a new job or a new role, you are learning. To know how you learn and maximize your ability is the key to your success.

For example, if, when you have completed the review given below, you discover that you learn best when you hear information then it will be helpful for you to create rhymes or songs that encompass the key facts you need to recall. You may also like to record information onto a tape and play it back so that you use both speaking and hearing.

Some people have 'interpersonal' intelligence, which means that they are able to communicate well with others and develop relationships. If you are a sociable person then it can help to learn in teams and share thoughts and ideas with others.

You may equally be someone who has physical intelligence – for example, you may be good at sport or dancing. You may therefore find it more effective and fun to do movement while you revise and learn. Try dancing around the room while you listen to information; or peg facts to stages of a daily journey, such as your journey from home to school.

A subject or task I have mastered	Subject/task:	What helped you? **Example: I was interested**
Subjects/tasks I find easy	Subject/task:	What helps you? **Example: I like big picture topics**
Subjects/tasks I find difficult	Subject/task:	What is the problem? **Example: I like more structured topics**
How can I motivate myself to persevere?	Ideas:	Who can help me? What helps me to study well? **Example: Being in my room listening to music**

Future Directions © Diane Carrington and Helen Whitten (Network Educational Press, 2005)

Exercise 3:3 Overviewing a book

This exercise enables people to overview a book and identify key points before they start to read it in detail. It helps to prioritize reading and also enhances recall and comprehension.

Aim To help the students learn and retain information effectively, for study, general knowledge and work.

Benefit Having a fast technique to overview and extract the key points from a book, report, journal or article is a skill that enables people to feel knowledgeable about a variety of topics. This technique empowers a person to gain the key points from a book in ten minutes rather than several hours. This raises confidence and capability.

Materials required:
- Each student needs to have one study book or a self-help or management book to work from. This must be laid out as a textbook with obvious section headings – not a work of fiction.
- Plain paper and pens

Session plan

1 Explain that reading and retaining key points from information is a skill that will stand them in good stead as they enter further education and the workplace.

2 Help each individual to consider how the eye and brain work when they read or observe a situation. For example, if they are reading a newspaper they are often able to pick up the main points in a very short time, but when they read for study they get 'serious' and try to get every detail, which only leads to stress. Help them think about how much the eye and the brain are processing even as they are sitting in the classroom – the details of the room, the colours, the other pupils, the subject. Much of this is happening on an unconscious basis.

3 Ask them to take two pieces of paper and tear them into bookmarks.

4 Explain that they are going to 'overview' their chosen book in ten minutes. This means that they will look at each page for one to two seconds per page. They will notice: chapter headings; section headings; diagrams; graphs; key points; how the book is structured and laid out; what sort of subjects the book is about; whether there are summaries at the end of the chapter or at the end of the book; the 'journey through the book'; the overall context and main points that seem to come out from the book.

5 Explain that they will not be taking notes as they go through the book but will put bookmarks into the pages that they find interesting and would want to read in detail.

6 Explain that they should not get drawn into reading the book – they should simply look for the general overview of what the book is about and not worry about details at this stage.

7 Help them to feel confident and relaxed about this process. Tell them to delete negative or doubting thoughts such as 'I don't think I can do this', and explain that the best learning results come when a person is relaxed but attentive.

8 Let them know that you will tell them when they are half-way through the exercise and also when they have two minutes left, at which time they can either go on to the end, if they are nearly there; or they can turn to the back of the book and work inwards as there are often useful pieces of information at the end of a book, such as summaries, appendices and index.

9 Start the ten-minute exercise.

10 Now ask them to Mind Map® the key points of the book as if they were going to give someone a general overview of what the book was about. Give them five to ten minutes to do the Mind Map®. They are allowed to refer back to the book and their bookmarks.

11 When they have finished, ask them to take their maps and tell another student about their book, and vice versa. Allow three to five minutes each way to share ideas.

12 Plenary:

- How did this exercise work?
- Did they get more or less than they expected from the book in ten minutes? (Usually people say more.)
- Can they see how this is a useful first step to any study or work reading?
- Can they see how this could also be a useful revision tool – for example, to overview any study or work book before an exam to gain the key points?
- How can they apply Mind Mapping® to study techniques?
- Explain that the overview exercise and the Mind Maps® provide excellent start-points to study; and also a fast-revision technique.
- How did it work to use the Mind Map® as a communication tool to tell another student about the book?
- Can they consider how they might share information between one another in this way in the future?

Overviewing a book

You are about to overview a book in ten minutes:

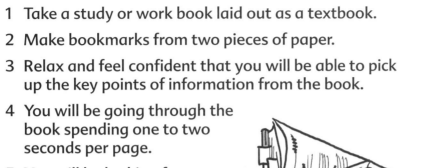

1   Take a study or work book laid out as a textbook.

2   Make bookmarks from two pieces of paper.

3   Relax and feel confident that you will be able to pick up the key points of information from the book.

4   You will be going through the book spending one to two seconds per page.

5   You will be looking for:
   • list of contents
   • chapter headings
   • section headings
   • general information about the book
   • diagrams, pictures and what they are about
   • summaries
   • key points of information.

6   You will not be reading the book or looking for details.

7   Do not worry about getting detailed facts or figures: this is a general overview exercise.

8   When you have gone through the book scanning each page, do a Mind Map® of key points. If you were to tell someone about this book what would you say was in it?

9   When you have finished your Mind Map® share this information with a classmate.

Applications of this exercise:

• You can use this exercise as a start-point for any study or work-related material.

• You can also use the overview exercise and Mind Mapping® for revision — in order to go through information and enhance your recall of a topic.

• You can use a Mind Map® for structuring an essay, project, dissertation or report before you write it in longhand.

Future Directions © Diane Carrington and Helen Whitten (Network Educational Press, 2005)

Mindpower: how the brain works

Six Tips

1 Where possible choose a study subject or career that excites you and plays to your strengths.

2 Give your brain a stretch into new areas: allow your brain to imagine and play – it aids learning and creativity.

3 Think positively about your ability to pick up and retain information. Thinking positively aids memory and success.

4 Repeat and practise new learning and new study techniques so that they become habits.

5 Capture information on maps and in graphic visual format, as this helps you to learn and remember information.

6 Practise overviewing a study or business book before reading it in detail. You can also use this technique for revising information before an exam or important meeting.

Why bother?

- You can halve your study time by using the overview technique with Mind Mapping®. You will also find it easier to remember information.

- These skills will help you achieve your goals and enable you to succeed in whatever capacity you choose.

- There are many opportunities available to you and feeling confident in your ability to learn, adapt and change to meet these situations is a key to your success.

My first action step

Commit yourself to one action in the next week that will help you to learn well and build new habits to support your future success.

This week I shall:

....

....

....

....

....

....

....

....

4 Building confidence

*When you are content to be simply yourself and don't compare
or compete, everybody will respect you.*

LAO TZU (6TH CENTURY BC)

As soon as you trust yourself, you will know how to live.

JOHANN WOLFGANG VON GOETHE (1749–1832)

CONFIDENCE SUPPORTS success in any field of endeavour. It helps each individual to think, communicate and learn. Confidence enables others to feel at ease and generates a feeling of trust.

Many people do not realize that they can develop the ability to feel confident by using the power of the mind, emotions and mental focus. This chapter explains this process and gives you some techniques for students to use in situations where they need to feel confident.

The benefits of building confidence

Developing self-confidence will help students in everything they do. It is easy for young people to criticize themselves – and each other – and take small mistakes and failures as evidence that they are 'no good'. Helping students to focus on the positives in their lives and the small achievements they have made enables them to develop self-esteem. This chapter builds on Chapters 1 and 2 and gives students specific thinking strategies to develop confidence and feel good about themselves in such situations as:

- taking exams;
- meeting people and developing relationships;
- first days at work;
- going to a party;
- a first date;
- making a presentation;
- running a seminar session;
- facing any challenge.

What the experts say

Self-confidence is the foundation stone of success. When people believe they can do something – or have the gut feeling that they can - they achieve results. As Henry Ford says 'If you think you can or if you think you can't, you are probably right!'. Successful business people, sports stars and actors comment that confidence and self-belief were the ingredients that drove them on through adversity to reach their goals.

Gaining this self-confidence has been the theme of many books. Timothy Gallwey in his books on the 'Inner Game' of various sports explains how achieving self-control and confidence on the sports field can be translated to many other life situations:

'As golfers undertake to play the Inner Game consciously and to develop skills of relaxed concentration, significant breakthroughs will follow. As a player learns to reduce the mental interference with his golf, he stands not only to reduce his golf handicap significantly, but also the ways in which he handicaps himself in the performance of every activity in his life. As he gains a measure of self-control he wins a measure of freedom.'

A story to share

A young girl called Sarah was doing very badly in class and was being disruptive. She had very little confidence in her ability to remember information – in fact, she could only remember about five history dates at one time. A new teacher arrived at her school and believed in her potential. She praised her efforts and recognized every small step she made. This gradually built Sarah's confidence and as her confidence developed so did her abilities. By the end of that term she was able to remember 30 history dates.

Three steps to building confidence

These are exercises to help students visualize, recall or imagine what it is like to feel confident. They will also identify what situations help to create confidence. Students will become aware that they can start to act confidently more frequently.

Exercise 4:1 Testimonials Log

This is a term's project where the students will keep a log of all praise and recognition they receive from other people – whether teachers, parents, siblings, family or peers.

Aim To help students open their minds to praise. Many people are given positive feedback but simply don't hear it. This exercise is designed to help them focus on the good things other people say to them.

Benefit Throughout their lives students will hear both critical and positive feedback about themselves. This feedback can relate to personal comments about themselves as individuals and to their performance at school or work. One of the common factors in underperformance, or demotivation, is that a person focuses only on negative comments. In the worst case this can lead to depression. If young people develop the ability to maintain balanced views of both positive and negative comments so that they can learn from them, they will gain a powerful lifelong strength.

Materials required:
• Photocopies of handout 4:1 and Six Tips for each individual
• A4 paper to make the Testimonials Log

Project

1 The process of logging praise can be started in a short exercise in the session or class to record any positive comments students may have heard in the past about themselves from parents, peers, teachers and others.

2 The students can then make keeping the Testimonials Log up to date a homework project.

3 They should keep the Log in their briefcase or bag for the whole term and continue to record positive feedback as they hear it.

4 Ask them to observe the process of feedback – how people give it; whether it is measured against the goal they were trying to achieve; whether they consider it fair and correct.

5 After a few weeks ask them to bring the Log into a session to get feedback.

6 Plenary:

- What was their experience?
- Did they become more aware of positive feedback?
- Did they become aware that the people giving them feedback have their own 'agendas', emotions and intentions?
- Just because one person says you are stupid does it make you stupid?
- Did focusing on the positives help them to feel more confident in studying a subject or coping with a specific situation?

Testimonials Log

As coaches, we find that many people ignore words of praise that other people give them and listen only to criticism. Dig back into your memory and record all the acknowledgement you have received.

1 Make a journal by stapling together about 12 A4 sheets.

2 Decorate the front sheet with the words 'Testimonials Log' and put your name on it.

3 Now cast your mind back to good things, praise and recognition that other people have given you in the past, for example:

   • applause for a school play;
   • good words in a school report;
   • incidental words of recognition from friends, family, teachers and others;
   • words of praise at the end of work assignments;
   • any good things ANYONE has said about you.

4 Jot these down on the second sheet of your Log.

5 Now make it a term project to keep your Log with you and note down any positive comment that you hear about yourself, either about yourself as a person or about your schoolwork, from teachers or from friends or family outside school.

6 Note down your comments regarding:

   • whether the person understood what you were trying to achieve when he or she gave you feedback;
   • whether you thought the person giving you positive feedback got pleasure from supporting you;
   • how easy you found it to accept positive feedback.

Future Directions © Diane Carrington and Helen Whitten (Network Educational Press, 2005)

Exercise 4:2 Acting confident

Through observing others, students can learn to notice the difference between the body language and voice tone of someone who is confident and someone who is not. This exercise gives the students an opportunity to look at famous people 'at their best and at their worst' and then also to act out the part of being confident. Through acting, students can begin to develop the experience of feeling more confident more of the time.

Aim To help students identify the recognizable ingredients of self-confidence.

Benefit By identifying the ingredients of confidence the students can begin to act as if they were confident.

Materials required:
- Photocopies of handout 4:2 and Six Tips for each individual
- Flip chart, whiteboard or paper to record ingredients of confidence

Session plan
1 Start with a general brainstorming session to discover which people the pupils consider to be confident. These may be people they know or public figures.
2 Help them to consider and identify how they know that these people are confident – is it clothes, voice, body language, status, position, the way others treat them?
3 Tell the students that they will now become actors and will be given some time to 'act' a scenario where they behave in a confident manner.
4 If working in a group, put them in groups of six and tell them that three of them have to be 'confident' and three of them have to be 'unconfident'. Suggest they create a scenario such as taking an unsatisfactory item back to a shop; giving a presentation; or going for an interview.
5 Give them ten minutes to prepare their improvisation and explain that they will need to identify characters and plot.
6 Each group then has five minutes to act out the scene.
7 Plenary:
   - What did they notice from the improvisations?
   - Could the audience tell which people were supposed to be the 'confident' ones? If so how did they tell?
   - What did it feel like to 'act' confident?
   - How could they use this in future?

Acting confident

In your groups decide:

Which people will act confident:

1 ....

2 ....

3 ....

Which people will act unconfident:

1 ....

2 ....

3 ....

The plot of your scenario:

Who are the characters?

....

....

What will they do?

....

....

What will be the problem in the scene?

....

....

What will be the outcome?

....

....

Future Directions © Diane Carrington and Helen Whitten (Network Educational Press, 2005)

Exercise 4:3 The self-confidence snapshot

This is a technique of mental focus whereby students can draw in the feeling of confidence just by imagining the sensory experience of how they feel when they are confident. They are able to consider situations where they feel confident and can then use this technique at any time.

Aim To give students a 'snapshot' of themselves that can be a mental tool to create self-confidence.

Benefit This is a model young people can use whenever there are difficult situations to face in the future. The 'confidence snapshot' is a life tool used by many sports people, actors, politicians and celebrities.

Materials required:
* Photocopies of handout 4:3 and Six Tips for each individual

Session plan
1 Explain that they can train their minds to remember what it feels like to be confident, as it is likely that they have experienced this at least once in their lifetime. It doesn't matter how long ago this was.
2 Explain that the 'confidence snapshot' can refer to them in either a home or a school environment – even at a party or on the sports field – as it is not the situation or place that is important but the feeling of being confident.
3 Get them to draw a picture of themselves feeling confident.
4 Ask them to caption the picture to help them recall the situation.
5 Finally, ask them to stand up, focus on feeling confident and demonstrate how they personally look and feel when they are confident. Do they stand taller? Do they smile? Do they walk more powerfully? How would people know?
6 Plenary:
   ■ Ask the students to share the situations in which they have previously felt confident.
   ■ Ask them to describe the different physiological feelings they experience when they are feeling confident –for example, standing taller, smiling, feeling 'lighter', feeling stronger.
   ■ Suggest they try to experience this feeling twice a day for the next week.

Confident snapshot

You can choose to be self-confident whenever you like:
1 Focus your mind, memory and attention.
2 Stop now and think about how you feel when you are feeling confident.
Do you stand taller? Breathe deeper? Smile more? What do you look like?
3 Create a mental snapshot of yourself feeling confident and
caption it with one word that will remind you of this feeling.
4 Think of a song or piece of music that helps you feel good.

Feel like?      Look like?

Thoughts?   Sounds?

The process

1 Remember an occasion when you felt self-confident. It doesn't matter where this was — it can be when you were at primary school winning a race on sports day, or when you did well in an exam or school play, or just when you were at home with your parents or friends, feeling good.

2 Use the power of your memory to recall the whole experience of how it felt to be confident.

3 Identify what your body feels like physically when you are confident — you usually are standing taller, more upright, feeling the strength of your body, breathing easily, feeling alert yet relaxed. Get this feeling now as you read.

4 Identify the whole emotional experience of self-confidence. How do you feel when you are confident? Get that feeling now.

5 Get a picture that reminds you of feeling confident — perhaps a place where something went well for you.

6 Now start to put the whole experience together. Draw a snapshot of yourself feeling confident either on the right or on another sheet of paper.

7 Put a caption to it with a word that will trigger the feeling of confidence.

Caption:..

Future Directions © Diane Carrington and Helen Whitten (Network Educational Press, 2005)

Building confidence

Six Tips

1 Be open to HEARING praise and recognition from others. Each day give yourself credit and think about the chance remarks or positive feedback you get from those around you.

2 If someone gives you a compliment, don't rubbish it but accept it with grace.

3 Notice and recognize your own successes and achievements. Even when you don't succeed, give yourself the credit for trying – that is a success and achievement in itself. Measure a person's feedback with your own honest viewpoint. Just because one person says you have not done well does not make it a 'fact' but simply their viewpoint; check back with your own measure.

4 Practise your 'self-confidence snapshot' routine every day – as many times as possible. Start to feel confident as you leave your bedroom in the morning, then again at breaktime, lunchtime, teatime and as you walk home. The more you practise the more natural a part of you confidence becomes. You can then use this technique any time you need to feel confident – exams, interviews, parties, dates and more ...

5 Listen to the stories of successful people on the television or read about them in magazines. You will often discover that they were not necessarily confident at the beginning of their lives but have developed confidence through hard work.

6 Notice your language. Are you putting yourself down – for example, 'I'm no good at this subject' or 'I will never be able to succeed at ...'?

Why bother?

- Confidence is the key to your own success and also to building successful relationships with others.
- A person who is confident has more inner security than someone who lacks confidence. This makes him or her more able to listen to the opinions and views of other people and not feel threatened by them.
- Confident people are more able to bring out the best in other people as well as themselves and be capable of building a supportive team of people around them.

My first action step

Commit yourself to one action step over the next week that will help you to build your confidence.

This week I shall:

....

....

....

....

....

Future Directions © Diane Carrington and Helen Whitten (Network Educational Press, 2005)

5 Developing emotional intelligence

Individuals ... are disturbed not by things but the views they take of them.
EPICTETUS, STOIC (AD100)

...There is nothing either good or bad, but thinking makes it so ... [Hamlet]
WILLIAM SHAKESPEARE (1564–1616)

MANAGING EMOTIONS is one of the hardest but most valuable skills to learn in life. If you can help young people to begin to understand how they can do this you will be giving them a head start in developing their relationships at home and at work.

Many of the problems that are affecting societies are the result of the inability to curb anger, frustration, stress and disappointment. The consequences can be actions that are immediately regretted, such as a road rage incident, or a fight in the playground, violence in a relationship, self-harm and breakdown.

We refer to this skill of emotional management as 'inside-out' personal leadership. That is because it starts with discipline of the mind. Everything that occurs inside the brain has consequences for communication, health, procrastination, body language, memory and more. Positive and constructive thoughts support success and achievement; negative thoughts deplete the ability to manage yourself or a situation.

Emotions are a part of everyday life but people don't have to be engulfed by them. The students can use them to their advantage to help motivate themselves to succeed. As they enter new environments they are likely to experience some different emotions. This chapter helps students to harness emotions so that they can manage new or difficult situations confidently.

The benefits of developing emotional intelligence

Emotional intelligence is not something that you learn and can then forget about. It is a lifetime process of self-awareness, self-observation and self-management. It can be hard work but the dividends are enormous. Emotional intelligence enables young people to make conscious decisions to avoid arguments, to stop bullying other people or allowing themselves to be bullied. It helps them to motivate themselves through difficult times such as revision, exams, interviews, redundancies, divorce, illness and more.

Managing emotions is a key lifeskill and can help with:

- self-motivation;
- the ups and downs of everyday life;

- empowering yourself to move forward from difficulty;
- managing and avoiding conflict;
- managing stress;
- understanding other people's behaviour;
- helping yourself and others to feel better;
- recognizing emotions and dealing with them in a constructive way;
- avoiding 'emotional hijack' where emotion overcomes reason.

What the experts say

With his book *Emotional Intelligence* Daniel Goleman (1996) has popularized the whole concept of emotional management. He argues that EI is a better determinant of success than professional qualifications. Most philosophers and psychologists have also argued that human beings seek happiness to avoid pain. Psychologist Robert Holden's work on 'The Happiness Factor' has demonstrated the very real health benefits of feeling happy.

Psychologists have realized that some people manage their emotions better than others and that this is generally due to how they choose to respond to the situation in which they find themselves. Even in such terrible conditions as a concentration camp or the kidnap experiences in Beirut, research has shown that while many people can experience the same events their individual responses are different.

We, the authors, have been trained in cognitive behavioural therapy and Neuro-Linguistic Programming, both of which provide measurable results to help individuals gain control over emotions, manage nerves and phobias, and learn how to develop strategies for overcoming everyday fears and problems. Research demonstrates that emotions influence decision making – people with damage to the emotional area of the brain are not good decision makers.

The expanding area of 'positive psychology' is leading psychologists to develop theories and techniques that help people to be more resilient to difficult events and experiences. These techniques enable people to realize that there is a part of the brain that controls their focus of attention and that they can either tune in to negative thoughts, expectations and emotions which lead to pain; or choose to tune in to positive thoughts, expectations and emotions which lead to happiness.

A story to share

A young girl had experienced frequent arguments with her older brother. Whenever he put her down she felt the need to answer back and got emotionally upset – either shouting at him or bursting into tears. Gradually she learned, with the help of her teacher, to control her emotions and take no notice of him.

She had been thinking: 'How dare he treat me this way!' And this had made her angry.

The teacher helped her to think: 'I would rather he did not treat me this way but I can manage it if he does and I can shrug my shoulders and leave the room.'

At first her brother tried to irritate her in other ways but when she did not rise to the bait he got bored and went off and played in his room with his friends. This made her life much easier and she felt happy.

Three steps to developing emotional intelligence

The exercises in this chapter all enable students to begin to consider what factors influence their emotional equilibrium. They are based on the principles of cognitive behavioural therapy, which supports the management of difficult situations and negative emotions through the demonstration that emotions are the consequences of beliefs, expectations and thoughts. Therefore by changing the thought the student can also change the emotion. The underlying philosophy is that 'individuals are disturbed not by events but by the response they take to those events'.

Exercise 5:1 Thoughts impact feelings

This exercise gives students the opportunity to stop and consider which situations they find emotionally challenging. They will learn about the step process from thought to emotion and how this influences behaviour. They are then asked to reflect on the thoughts underlying the emotions that they experienced in certain situations. This helps them to tune into their emotions and become aware of what is causing them.

Aim To help students become aware of their inner voice – the 'thinking' that goes on inside their heads – and how this impacts their emotions. They need particularly to notice negative thinking and realize that they have the ability to transform this into constructive thinking in order to make their emotions work well for them.

Benefit Managing the thinking process enables students to choose their emotional state in any situation, good or bad.

Materials required:
- Photocopies of handout 5:1 (see *www.networkpress.co.uk/resources* for colour version) and Six Tips for each individual
- Flip chart, whiteboard or paper to demonstrate the thought-changing process

Session plan

1 Help the students consider what emotions are and brainstorm some situations where they have experienced emotions – 'I felt angry when …' 'I felt happy when …' 'I felt upset when …'

2 Explain that an 'inner' thinking voice is perfectly normal and that everyone experiences this.

3 Explain that we can sometimes appear to have several different voices, or aspects of us, talking at once – for example, one part of us might want to eat chocolate but the other 'voice' reminds us that we want to stay slim and healthy. Another example might be going into an exam where one part of us feels confident that we know enough to pass and the other part of us makes us doubt this. This generally results in stress.

4 Explain that the first part of the process towards emotional intelligence is to become aware (a) of emotions experienced in different situations and (b) the thinking that inspires those emotions.

5 You can then explain that there is part of the brain we can call the 'Controller' that allows them to make a choice regarding which voice they listen to and focus on – so this system will help them to change thoughts and therefore emotions. This is demonstrated in the handout.

6 Plenary:
- Could they give an example of a situation where negative thinking created negative emotions?
- How can they use this awareness?

Thoughts impact emotions

Stress affects the brain

Situation

Thoughts → Emotions → Behaviour

"I can't cope"

Anxiety
Anger

Decision making
Communicating
Procrastinating

1 Wiring the brain

"I can't manage
this situation"

2 Thinking habits

"I can't manage
this situation"

Stress
hormones
released

3 Switching the circuitry

"I can't —
it won't work"

"I can —
it may work"

4 Accentuate the positive, eliminate the negative!

"I can —
it will work"

Endorphins
released

The inner voice

Identify two difficult situations. Write down (1) the situation, (2) the emotion you experienced in that situation, (3) identify the thought you were having that might have inspired negative emotion and (4) a positive alternative.

Situation	Emotion	Negative thought	Positive alternative
1			
2			

Future Directions © Diane Carrington and Helen Whitten (Network Educational Press, 2005)

Exercise 5:2 Expectations impact emotions

Expectations of a situation or of a person can cause both negative and positive emotions. If one expects too much of oneself, another person or a situation then this can lead to stress, disappointment, resentment and anger. The converse is also true. This exercise allows the students to share experiences of how expectations of a situation have influenced their emotional state.

Aim To help students understand how distorted expectations influence emotions.

Benefit To enable students to develop rational expectations of themselves, others and situations in general.

Materials required:
• Photocopy of Six Tips for each individual
• Paper and pens

Session plan

1 Share some ideas and thoughts about how expectations shape emotions, for example:

> If you expected your parents to give you £50 for a Christmas present and they gave you only £25 then you might feel disappointed or stressed because the expectation had been 'they should have given me £50'. If, on the other hand, you had expected to be given only £25 and then your parents gave you £50 you would have felt delighted as your expectation had been exceeded.

> Using cases such as the following, explain how a person can make a situation worse than it really is through having a distorted and personal expectation of it:

>   ■ An expectation of oneself might be: 'I *should* have got a B++ but I only got a B– for my project so I am no good.' This could lead to depression or anxiety.

>   ■ An expectation of another person might be: 'I would do this task this way – so they *should* do it the same way or they are stupid!' This could lead to frustration or anger.

>   ■ An expectation of a situation might be: 'There *should* be silence in the library because otherwise I can't concentrate and if there isn't silence then that is an awful situation that I can't manage.' This could lead to anxiety and resentment of those making a noise.

2 Allow them ten minutes in groups of four to identify personal situations where their expectations have led to raised emotions. Suggest they consider whether their original expectation was reasonable or distorted in the circumstances.

3 Ask them to develop some thoughts as to how they might manage this type of situation in future.

4 Plenary:

> Discuss their findings.
>   ■ Could they give an example of where their own expectation of themselves had led them to feel stupid or stressed or demotivated?
>   ■ Could they give an example of where their own expectation of how something should be done, or how to communicate, had led them to feel angry or disappointed with another person?

- Could they change their thinking and the language in their heads to make themselves feel better in such situations?
- How can they apply this understanding in future?

Exercise 5:3 TCP – thoughts, circumstances and physiology

The TCP Model is designed to help pupils manage their emotions by changing three things: **thoughts, circumstances, physiology**. Emotions have immediate physical consequences and affect cognitive ability and health. For this reason it is advisable to manage stress and negative emotions in situations where clear thinking is required – for example, in an exam or interview. The physiology of emotion is individual. What is helpful to realize is that by changing physiology – for example, by relaxing tension in neck and shoulders, or breathing slowly – emotions change also.

Aim   To demonstrate that thoughts, circumstances and physiology all influence emotional equilibrium and can be altered to help manage any situation or event.

Benefit   This is a model for their confidence toolkit. It is a way to ensure that they manage their emotions and give of their best.

Materials required:
- Photocopies of handout 5:3 and Six Tips for each individual
- Flip chart, whiteboard or paper to capture constructive thoughts and ideas

Session plan
1   Introduce the TCP Model, give them the handouts and explain how stress works.
2   Explain that we have the capacity to change our **thoughts** and expectations in any situation; the **circumstances** of situations – for example, where a meeting takes place, what you wear, what time of day suits you best; personal **physiology** – for example, standing taller, relaxing the shoulders, breathing deeply or smiling can alter emotions.
3   Take an example situation, say going into an exam – or any situation the students suggest.
4   Write the situation on the board or on paper and then ask the students to suggest positive and constructive thoughts that would help them manage the situation.
5   Now ask them to offer suggestions for specific practical circumstances that would help them manage – for example, being able to attend two meetings close together geographically.
6   Now ask them what physiology might help – for example, deep breathing into the diaphragm rather than shallow breathing. If possible, once you have captured these ideas on the board or on paper, ask them to stand up and show you how their physiology will help them. Get them to tense and feel nervous or angry at first; then ask them just to change their physiology and see and feel the difference this makes.
7   Explain that emotional management can help them achieve their goals. For example, when they put a date in their diary for an event that may raise emotions they can choose the emotion that would most support them in the circumstance and use the TCP Model to plan their emotional state alongside planning the task itself.
8   Plenary:
   - What is their understanding of emotional intelligence and how it can be applied?
   - When can they use the TCP Model?
   - How could this Model help them manage their own emotions?
   - How might it also help them to manage raised emotions in other people?
   - Can they give examples of how their thinking or expectations have raised emotions?

TCP – thoughts, circumstances, physiology

This Model helps you to understand that thoughts, circumstances and physiology all influence your emotional equilibrium. You can use TCP to help you to make the most of each situation you face.

THOUGHTS

Negative thoughts show in body language. In an instant, you have less physical presence and are less capable of putting your point of view with any conviction because negative thinking causes stress. Negative thoughts literally incapacitate you. Whether you are walking into an exam or an interview, it is important to ensure that thoughts support your goals.

Identifying negative thoughts
Meeting someone for the first time or going to an interview you might think:

'Why should they want to see me?'
'I am no good anyway.'
'I have nothing to offer.'

Changing to positive thoughts
Counteract doubts and create constructive thoughts:

'They have invited me here so they obviously want to see me.'
'I am unique.'
'I have got lots to offer and I can learn.'

CIRCUMSTANCES
You can sometimes take control of circumstances — for example, what you wear, what time of day a meeting starts and where it is held. Always check whether it is possible to identify the circumstances that most support your goals.

PHYSIOLOGY
Moving physically changes your emotions and can release chemical substances in your body called endorphins, which are believed to promote a feeling of well-being and help you to relax. Notice the different sensations you experience during difficult situations — for example, does your body feel different, do you breathe differently, do you stand differently, do you speak differently? Become aware of what your own personal emotional signals are. Some people get butterflies in their tummies when they are nervous. What do you get?

If you are angry you can relax your neck and shoulders and it will relax your emotions. If you are tense and anxious you can stand taller, breathe deeper and smile and this will help you to feel more confident.

The TCP Model

Throughout your life you will always experience emotions. Your emotions give you important signals about your life and decisions. Learning to recognize, acknowledge and value how you are feeling enables you to become in tune and comfortable with yourself. You become capable of listening to what those emotions are telling you and then choosing what you do about it and how you feel. You can then channel your emotions in a positive way.

We shall develop emotional intelligence further in Chapter 6, **Managing stress**.

Applying TCP — 3 Changes

• Change your
  - Thinking
  - Circumstances
  - Physiology

Future Directions © Diane Carrington and Helen Whitten (Network Educational Press, 2005)

Developing emotional intelligence

Six Tips

1 Chart the emotions you experience in the next week. Write down what made you feel happy, angry, sad, frustrated and so on.

2 Try to understand what other people might be feeling and build empathy.

3 Think of a goal you are trying to achieve and choose an appropriate emotion to support you getting there.

4 Your brain produces mental images. Using your imagination, visualize yourself approaching a situation in a more powerful way – see yourself standing taller and managing your emotions positively.

5 Learn to comfort yourself and recognize what you need to do to feel better.

6 Practise physical movement or exercise to shift you out of unhelpful feelings. For example, stretch and open your arms, go for a walk or dance!

Why bother?

- Emotional intelligence can be helpful – for example, to transform feelings such as anger, nerves, helplessness.

- You can use emotional intelligence to manage difficult situations; when something goes wrong, you can help yourself feel better.

- In specific situations such as exams, interviews, meetings, presentations and dates you can start the situation off by drawing in a positive emotion – by choice.

- If you experience conflict or someone does something that annoys you, you can stop and think about the consequences of action. Use the TCP Model to manage the situation in a calm manner.

My first action step

Commit yourself to one action step over the next week that will help you to develop emotional intelligence.

This week I shall:

....

....

....

....

....

....

....

6 Managing stress

If you are distressed by anything external, the pain is not due to the thing itself, but to your estimate of it; and this you have the power to revoke at any moment.

MARCUS AURELIUS ANTONINUS (AD121–180)

STRESS CAN DEBILITATE, and undermine performance and communication. It can also lead to long-term illness if not addressed in good time. To help students develop the ability to manage their stress at an early stage of life will have a beneficial impact on health and happiness as well as results.

With the technological advances of recent years people are finding themselves increasingly in demand 24/7. This has led to what is called the 'intensification' of work, where many people feel that they have to produce results in a very short timespan and deal with a wide variety of tasks. Travel to work can be difficult; and people worry about job security as well as feeling under pressure to meet financial demands.

We covered the topic of emotional intelligence in Chapter 5. This chapter aims to explore the causes and symptoms of stress and help students to develop skills and strategies to manage stressful situations.

The benefits of managing stress

Stress makes you stupid – it cuts off the 'thinking' part of the brain and switches people into survival mode. Managing stress in situations such as exams, driving tests, interviews or personal conflict can support health and good relationships. Long-term stress can cause debilitating illness and undermine confidence and self-esteem.

People can become aware of their own physical and behavioural symptoms of stress and take action before their health is impaired. Building self-resilience to the ups and downs of life enables students to remain calm and confident in difficult situations.

What the experts say

In an HSE survey in 2004, over half a million individuals in Britain believed that they were experiencing work-related stress at a level that was making them ill. Nearly one in five of all working individuals thought their job was very or extremely stressful. These studies indicated that people first became aware of work-related stress in the 12 months before they became ill. It has resulted in an estimated 13 million lost working days per year.

Stress depletes the immune system. Recent research shows that many illnesses are caused by stress and doctors now understand the physical chemistry of stress and its impact on health and behaviour. Psychoneuroimmunology is a field where clinicians study the impact of stress and negative thinking on health. There is a body of research that shows that lowering stress through active positive visualization can shorten the length of time it takes for a person to recover from an illness. For example, an ordinary skin cut can take four days longer to heal if the person is stressed.

The development of cognitive behavioural therapy has been proven to relieve stress and enable people to live satisfying and fulfilling lives. Psychologists have spent years studying neurosis but it is only recently that psychology is moving towards giving people 'preventive' models and strategies so that they can maintain emotional equilibrium despite external factors.

A story to share

Brian was a young manager in a business. He was doing extremely well and his department had reached its targets the previous year. This put pressure on Brian to ensure that he achieved those targets again the following year and he started to work even harder to reach his goals.

At the same time his girlfriend broke off their relationship and he took this as a personal failure. The influence of a very dominant father drove Brian to 'prove' himself at work, and this helped him to manage the rejection he had faced in his private life.

He was very intelligent and capable, and it never occurred to him that he might be someone who would suffer from stress. His boss and colleagues gave him more and more projects and tasks to complete because he was so efficient, and Brian began to work late. He started a relationship with a new girlfriend, which put him under pressure to take her out to restaurants and added some financial strain.

On the evenings he spent at home alone, he was too tired to cook himself a meal so he would order an unhealthy takeaway and fall asleep in front of the television. When he went to bed he found himself waking in the night and worrying.

One day a project he had been working on went wrong and he collapsed in tears in his office. His boss was amazed, as he had thought that Brian was so capable and strong. Brian said 'I can't take any more'.

He had not recognized how stress was building up. Each small pressure adds to the 'pressure cooker' of stress chemistry in the body and at some point this can explode if not handled well. Brian had to take three months off work and learn through counselling how to take better care of himself in the future.

Three steps to managing stress

The three exercises in this chapter will give students some theory and information about stress and also help them to identify their own causes and symptoms so that they can take action before stress has taken too great a toll on them mentally or physically. Explain to them that practising these techniques can bring tangible benefits to their lives in health, happiness and mental focus.

Exercise 6:1 Identifying and reframing the causes of stress

This exercise enables the students to realize that each stressful situation is just a problem to be solved. One way of easing pressure is to 'reframe' the way you look at the situation and consider how it may be seen in a positive light.

Aim To help students identify the factors that cause them stress and to approach the situations more positively.

Benefit Unless people are aware of what is causing them stress they cannot take action to remedy the situation. This exercise helps students take the first step towards problem solving.

Materials required:
- Photocopies of handout 6:1 (see *www.networkpress.co.uk/resources* for colour version) and Six Tips for each individual
- Flip chart, whiteboard or paper to capture stressful situations

Session plan
1 Introduce the topic of stress.
2 Explain that stress causes ill-health and impairs the natural cognitive functions of the brain. This causes huge loss of productivity in British business as well as a drain on the National Health Service. On a personal level it can disrupt good relationships and enjoyment of life.
3 Remind them that previous chapters (specifically Chapter 5 on emotional intelligence) explained that it is a person's response to a situation that causes stress, not the situation itself.
4 Ask the students to work in pairs on the handout and record their own 'pressure points' on the map. Explain that the branches are suggestions and they may have additional ideas that are more relevant.
5 Once they have spent ten minutes in their pairs talking about their personal causes of stress, suggest that they look at their map and give each item a priority number: 10 = high stress; 1 = low stress. This will help them to identify the factors that most need dealing with in their lives and explore what to do about them.
6 Once they have discussed this in pairs, encourage the group to share the type of situations that cause them stress and record these on the board or on paper. Circle in red those that they feel are the worst stress factors. Inevitably, there may be some sensitive issues here, so it may be valuable to ensure that you have some links and further sources of reference for them if necessary.
7 Finally, explain that transforming stressful situations takes creativity and a 'positive' viewpoint. If possible, raise the energy of the room and ask the students to 'reframe' some of the situations in a positive light. For example, 'sitting on a bus in a traffic jam' could be seen as 'an opportunity to listen to a personal stereo, or read a book'. Or 'moving to a new city' could be 'an opportunity to meet new friends'.
8 Plenary:
    - Are there some common experiences of what causes stress?
    - What are some of the consequences of being stressed?
    - Are there some stress factors that they need to accept will not change (for example, certain regulations at school) and could they accept this rather than allow themselves to get stressed?
    - How might they 'reframe' stressful situations in the future so that they can manage to think more positively and not get too 'hooked into' a problem?

Pressure points: causes of stress

Reflect on your life at home and at school and use the map to record some of the 'pressure points' that are causing you stress at the moment. If possible, work in pairs and see if you share some of the same problems.

The branches on the map are just suggestions — you may have other topics you want to add instead. This is fine.

When you have filled in the whole map then prioritize which pressure points cause you most stress and which cause you least and give each a number, with 10 being high stress and 1 being low stress.

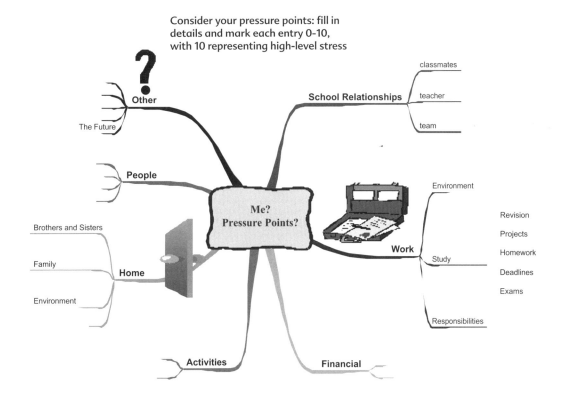

Consider your pressure points: fill in details and mark each entry 0-10, with 10 representing high-level stress

Once you have prioritized your pressure point problems you can start to consider how you might resolve some of the situations that are causing you stress. One way to do this is to build on the models we used in Chapter 5 on emotional intelligence and start to 'reframe' the problems in a positive light. How might you see these situations in a positive way? Write some ideas and actions below:

....

....

....

....

Future Directions © Diane Carrington and Helen Whitten (Network Educational Press, 2005)

Exercise 6:2 Fight or flight? Noticing personal symptoms of stress

This exercise gives the students information about the physical and behavioural symptoms they might experience when they are stressed.

Aim To demonstrate that there are both physical and behavioural symptoms of stress and to help students identify their own symptoms so that they can take prompt action.

Benefit Taking action to manage stress at an early stage relieves the problems long-term stress can cause to health, performance and relationships.

Materials required:
- Photocopies of handouts 6:2:1 and 6:2:2 (see *www.networkpress.co.uk/resources* for colour versions) and Six Tips for each individual
- Flip chart, whiteboard or paper to record actions

Session plan

1 Explain that the body's response to stress produces physical symptoms. You introduced them to the effects of stress and negative thinking on the brain and body in Chapter 5 on emotional intelligence, so refer them back to the negative thinking spiral.

2 Give them handout 6:2:1 and explain that when a person is stressed the body releases noradrenalin, adrenalin and cortisol to prepare the body for the 'fight or flight' response – to give the person strength to fight or speed to run.

3 Explain that these chemicals are effective in giving a person strength or speed but that long-term cortisol depletes the immune system and leads to illness and physical symptoms of stress.

4 Ask them to share in groups of four some of the physical symptoms they have experienced in their own lifetimes.

5 Take some feedback and explain that the body has an intelligence of its own and is bringing stress to the person's attention through these physical symptoms. Explain that it is therefore important that they become observant of their own physiology. If they find themselves constantly getting colds and flu, or digestive problems, they should consider whether these illnesses could be stress related. They should think about anything that is causing them stress and devise some solutions to solve those problems. Give them five to ten minutes to discuss this.

6 Give them handout 6:2:2 and explain that when chemicals build up in the body as a response to stress they affect the nervous system and lead to changes of behaviour.

7 Ask them to consider, in their groups of four, which of them are fight-mode people (who become impatient, intolerant and aggressive) and which are flight-mode people (who retreat into themselves, become quiet and antisocial). Give them five to ten minutes to discuss this.

8 Plenary:
   - Take some feedback and ask them if they have noticed instances of stress-related behaviour in themselves and their friends in the past.
   - Ask them to identify behaviours that indicate that a person is stressed.
   - Ask them how they might ensure that they identify both their physical and behavioural responses more easily in future.
   - How can they look out for one another and help each other identify stress causes and symptoms?
   - What can they do to take preventive action to avoid stress in future?

The physiology of stress

Fight or flight response — stress makes us stupid!

Pupils dilate for better vision

Adrenalin or noradrenalin released

Lungs take in more oxygen

Digestion halts

Circulatory system diverts blood from non-essential functions to muscles and brain

Brain perceives threat — hippocampus activates

Brain dulls sense of pain

Cortisol released

Blood pressure and heart rate soar

Liver pours out glucose

Fat reserves processed for energy

= Strength or speed

Symptoms of stress

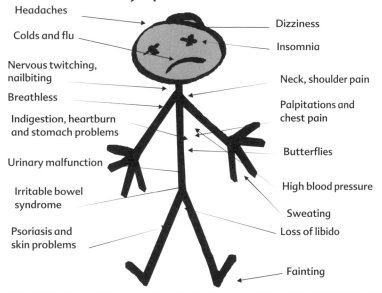

Headaches

Colds and flu

Nervous twitching, nailbiting

Breathless

Indigestion, heartburn and stomach problems

Urinary malfunction

Irritable bowel syndrome

Psoriasis and skin problems

Dizziness

Insomnia

Neck, shoulder pain

Palpitations and chest pain

Butterflies

High blood pressure

Sweating

Loss of libido

Fainting

Long-term health effects

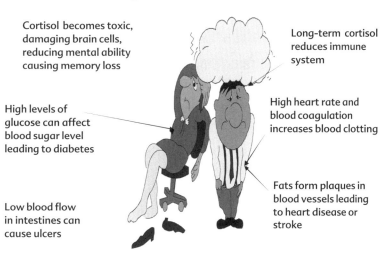

Cortisol becomes toxic, damaging brain cells, reducing mental ability causing memory loss

High levels of glucose can affect blood sugar level leading to diabetes

Low blood flow in intestines can cause ulcers

Long-term cortisol reduces immune system

High heart rate and blood coagulation increases blood clotting

Fats form plaques in blood vessels leading to heart disease or stroke

Behavioural symptoms of stress

Behaviour Changes — Stage One

- The Hurry Pattern!
- Loss of sense of humour
- Not eating properly
- Time pressures — less social
- Foot tapping
- Making mistakes, missing deadlines
- Increased alcohol consumption

Behaviour Changes — Stage Two

- Memory loss, poor concentration
- Slamming desk drawers
- Anxious, demoralized
- Lack of confidence, low esteem
- Over-working, long hours
- Difficulty sleeping, waking early
- Impatient and intolerant

Behaviour Changes — Stage Three

- Constantly tired, loss of energy
- Difficulty making decisions
- Tearful, unable to cope
- Burnout
- Clinical depression

Future Directions © Diane Carrington and Helen Whitten (Network Educational Press, 2005)

Exercise 6:3 Time and prioritization model

This model helps students to identify the most important factors in their lives so that they can consider which activities support their emotional equilibrium.

Aim To help the students understand that planning and prioritization of time can relieve stress.

Benefit Learning to manage time at an early age can help students to plan revision time, manage priorities at school, home and work, and gain balance of life.

Materials required:
- Photocopies of handout 6:3 and Six Tips for each individual
- Flip chart, whiteboard or paper for the warm-up and for recording key messages

Session plan
1 Explain that every person has the same amount of time to manage – 24 hours in each day. Successful people manage time effectively, focusing on priority activities and priority relationships, and do not get distracted by the less important tasks. Equally, they do not procrastinate over tasks they know need doing.
2 If the setting is appropriate, ask the students to go up to the flip chart or whiteboard, otherwise use paper, and record one task they usually procrastinate over – a task they do not like to do.
3 Ask them to list on another flip chart or whiteboard, or on paper, the activities they tend to do instead of the activity they should be doing. These are 'displacement' activities that postpone achievement of goals.
4 Have a brief discussion about what this means and how it impacts their lives.
5 Now give them the handout and ask them to list the key relationships and activities they need to focus on at home and at work. Suggest they divide the circle into three or more chunks – for example, 'Home', 'School/Work', 'Leisure' – and list priority activities and relationships in each. Allow five to ten minutes for this exercise.
6 If time, ask them to share their lists with a partner to see if there are any common priorities.
7 Plenary:
    - Were there any common activities that they tended to postpone?
    - If so, why did they want to avoid them?
    - Were there any common displacement activities?
    - Before this lesson, had they ever considered what was most important to them?
    - Will this make them undertake tasks in a different order in future?
    - What impact might this have on their lives?

Time and prioritization

Your time is like a cake. You can divide it up into chunks. What you want to ensure is that you focus on what matters most to you. Spend time on the most important chunks first and leave the less important activities to the last. Divide the circle below into chunks representing the activities and relationships that you consider are your priorities at home and at school.

At School/Work ask yourself: what is the best use of my mind and attention?

At Home and Leisure ask yourself: who and what is most important to me?

School/Work	Home	Leisure
1	1	1 ....
2	2	2 ....
3	3	3 ....
4	4	4 ....
5	5	5 ....
6	6	6 ....

Managing stress

Six Tips

1 Take control of your time – plan your time and focus on what matters most to you and your future success and happiness.

2 Notice what situations cause you stress and realize that you can take action to solve these challenges.

3 Become aware of your physical and behavioural symptoms of stress and take action to manage your stress so that you do not risk burnout.

4 Try to recognize potentially stressful situations involving others and take steps to avoid them, returning later when things have calmed down.

5 Apply what you have learned in other chapters to help you manage stress – for example, the thinking models from Chapter 5, *Emotional intelligence*; and the meditation models you will be given in Chapter 18, *Understanding the inner self*.

6 Don't try to be superman or superwoman – be discerning about what you take on and how you spend your time. Ask for help if necessary.

Why bother?

■ Stress is debilitating and makes you stupid! It shuts off the thinking part of your brain and pushes you into survival mode of 'fight or flight'. This makes you fuzzy-headed, less articulate and unable to recall information.

■ If you ignore stress symptoms you can find yourself getting sick more often as stress impairs your immune system. In the long term, stress can make you seriously ill.

■ When you are stressed you make bad decisions and do not communicate effectively.

My first action step

Commit yourself to one action step over the next week that will help you to manage stress.

This week I shall:

....

....

....

....

....

....

....

7 Understanding communication skills

*The greatest compliment that was ever paid me was when someone asked me
what I thought, and attended to my answer.*

HENRY DAVID THOREAU (1817–1862)

*We have two ears and only one tongue in order that
we may hear more and speak less.*

DIOGENES (412–322 BC)

IN THIS CHAPTER we consider various communication skills, which will equip students with a range of techniques to adopt in various situations. If they master communication skills while they are at school it will be very straightforward for them to use such skills appropriately when they enter the world of work.

Young people communicate every day with their peers, their friends, their family and their teachers. However, they often feel disempowered in their communications with adults. They can find it difficult to express themselves in a calm rational way and may alternate between being submissive and then aggressive. Acting in an assertive way requires different techniques for young people, when they have to demonstrate respect and understanding of the rules, but also want to make their point heard.

Assertiveness is a very complex issue. Although it is clearly acknowledged that the most valuable and productive way to act is assertively it is without a doubt not straightforward for students. In school situations, rules have to be obeyed and relationships cannot be equal. The power is unmistakably with the teacher and the students must recognize this. However, it is to the benefit of all if the student does not behave aggressively, disrupting the class, or passively accept things in a subservient way. Therefore it is imperative that the teacher encourages the students all to act in an assertive a way as possible in appropriate situations. It is recognizing these appropriate situations that many young people find the most difficult challenge. This way of behaving will also be most beneficial when they leave school and enter the world of work. It encourages mutual respect, regardless of the power relationship. At work, they will again meet and have to deal with different power relationships, and having the skills to recognize them and to cope with them will be invaluable.

The benefits of understanding communication skills

As human beings are social creatures, mastering the art of communication will be a useful skill for students throughout their lives. In the future they will find themselves in many different situations where they will need to employ a range of different communication skills, from formal interviews to working in diverse teams.

Understanding both the subtleties and the repercussions of their communications will enable them to adopt appropriate techniques.

In appreciating that communication is a two-way process – requiring a sophisticated use of the correct language, spoken in the appropriate way, and the ability to really listen to exactly what is being said – students will be able to relate to others more effectively. This will give them the ability to hear accurately what others are saying to be heard themselves.

What the experts say

The art of communication involves many complicated processes, many of which have been discussed earlier. To be able to communicate confidently, people need to have an understanding of themselves, to recognize their own strengths and weaknesses and not assume that others are necessarily going to act in a certain way. They can then avoid incorrect assumptions, which make true understanding impossible.

Much research has been undertaken into the importance of developing an understanding both of our own communication style and that of others. Israel, Whitten and Shaffran (2000) emphasize this when they say: 'To manage your own career you need to understand your present communication style and develop successful working relationships with a diverse group of clients and colleagues.' This skill is also essential at school, college and when seeking a job, and to accomplish it we need to develop both speaking and listening skills.

Listening is often very difficult to do well and people are seldom taught how to do it. Our brains have a very short attention span and are always eager to jump to conclusions, or to fill in the missing word. Unless we are consciously concentrating, we automatically insert words, make assumptions and therefore reach incorrect conclusions. Many misunderstandings arise because of this. How many problems begin with comments such as: 'I thought you meant...' or 'I thought you said...'?

Another possible area of confusion in communication is the use of stereotyping. People use stereotypes in their day-to-day lives to simplify the world; television soap operas and advertisements use them all the time to speak in shorthand to their audiences. Young people are particularly frequent and sophisticated users of this medium and are often quick to make judgements based on what someone looks like or how they sound, disregarding what is actually being said.

Communication happens all the time. An easy way to introduce this to students is to set them this question:

Which of the following is a form of communication?
a) Avoiding eye contact as you buy something in a shop.
b) Standing in a corner in a crowded room with your arms folded.
c) Talking to someone.
d) All of the above.

If you chose d), you are absolutely correct.

A story to share

Jo always ended up in trouble. Other people made comments about their teachers, but whenever Jo said anything a teacher seemed to hear immediately and pick on him. Jo wouldn't have minded if he had felt that the punishments were fair and just, but on most occasions teachers seemed to overreact and to set out to annoy him.

One teacher in particular always gave him a hard time. Even when Jo tried to get on with his work the teacher stood next to him and stared at him in an intimidating way, putting him off. The minute Jo looked up the teacher made a sarcastic comment. Jo immediately made an even more sarcastic comment back and the class laughed, so Jo was sent out of the room and had to do a detention.

One day, Jo decided to act differently. When the teacher made a sarcastic comment Jo ignored him. This happened on three occasions and each time Jo ignored him. At the end of the lesson Jo got up and walked out with his friends.

Who had won?

Three steps to understanding communication skills

These games and exercises demonstrate the importance of clear communication and help students to improve their questioning and listening techniques. If working outside a class you can play a role yourself, but, where possible, try to do these exercises in a small group.

Exercise 7:1:1 Three short communication games

By participating in these games, students experience first hand the feelings of frustration caused by bad communication.

Aim To demonstrate the need for clear precise instructions and the benefits of real two-way communication.

Benefit Often, describing a situation does not have the same impact as experiencing it, and these games give the students the opportunity to see what it feels like to experience bad communication.

Materials required:
• Photocopies of handouts 7:1:1 (i) and 7:1:1 (ii) and Six Tips for each individual
• Pens and plain paper
• Whiteboard or paper to record learning

Session plan
1 Introduce the importance of clear, precise instructions and explain that in order to introduce this topic they are first going to have the opportunity to experience different types of communication.
2 Undertake the games.

Game one
Ask them to sit back to back in pairs (A and B).
Pupil A is given handout 7:1:1 (i) and describes the drawing to pupil B (who must not be shown the handout).

B is not allowed to ask questions and must remain silent.

B tries to draw the object that A is describing. Allow two minutes.

Then swop over. B describes the object on handout 7:1:1(ii) for A to draw.

Feedback:

- Ask A and B how it felt.

- What hindered them?

- What would have helped?

- How are real-life conversations like this?

Game two

Ask them to work in groups of three.

One is to be the Speaker, one is to be the Listener, one is to be the Observer.

The Speaker tells the Listener about a television programme or a book he or she really likes.

The Listener is quiet, asks no questions, makes no eye contact, looks away.

The Observer watches and listens and notes, on plain paper, how he or she thinks the Listener and Speaker feel.

Feedback:

- Ask the Speaker, Listener and Observer to give feedback individually.

- Ask the Speaker and Listener how they felt.

- Ask the Observer what he or she observed.

- What hindered them?

- What would have helped?

- How are real-life conversations like this?

Game three

Ask them to work in groups of three.

One is to be the Speaker, one is to be the Listener, one is to be the Observer.

The Speaker tells the Listener about a film or some music he or she really likes.

The Listener does NOT listen and tells the Speaker about a film or music that he or she really likes.

Each person continues to put forward his or her own points, without listening to the other. (Tell them to try not to shout over one another but just wait for one to finish before switching the subject back to what they want to talk about.)

The Observer watches and listens.

Let the groups change roles, if time permits.

Feedback:

- Ask the Speaker, Listener and Observer to give feedback individually.

- Ask the Speaker and Listener how they felt.

- Ask the Observer what he or she observed.

- What hindered them?

- What would have helped?

- How are real-life conversations like this?

3. Plenary:

- What did the pupils gain from these exercises?

- Can they think of any real-life examples of these experiences?

- Will they act differently in the future?

- If so, in what way?

Communication games

Describe this picture to your partner for him or her to draw.

You are NOT allowed to show your partner the picture or to see what he or she is drawing.

Your partner is not allowed to ask you any questions.

Good luck!

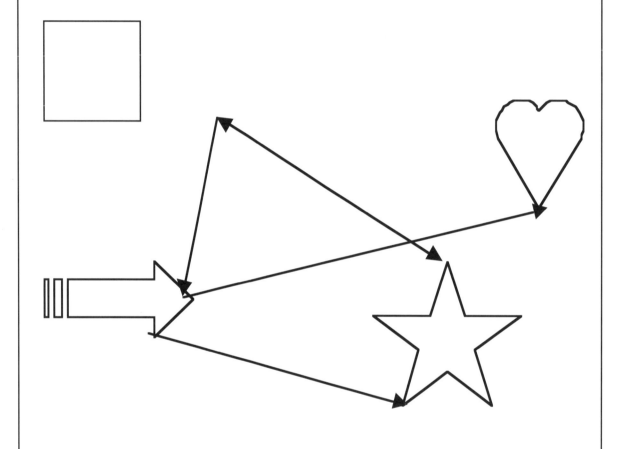

Communication games

Describe this picture to your partner for him or her to draw.

You are NOT allowed to show your partner the picture or to see what he or she is drawing.

Your partner is not allowed to ask you any questions.

Good luck!

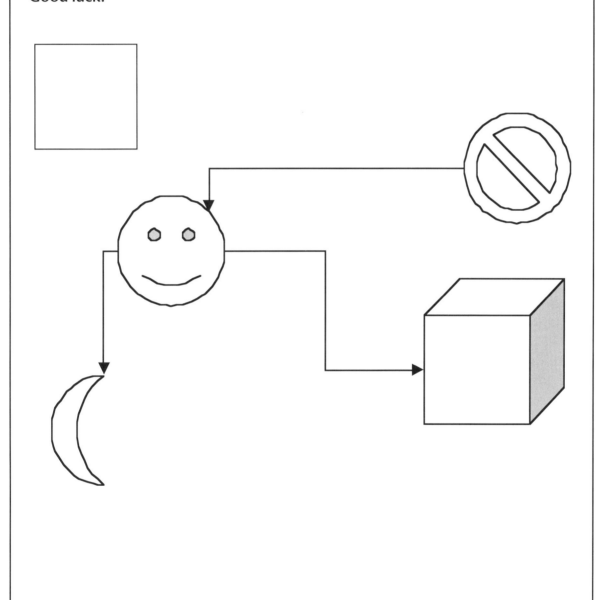

Exercise 7:1:2 Active listening

This exercise requires the students to work in small groups, to analyse the different elements of communication in different situations and to decide on the appropriate type of questioning required to obtain accurate information.

Aim To highlight the components of active listening and give the students the opportunity to use and to practise these skills.

Benefit By using the skills, the students will be able to appreciate how using a range of questions can help them to understand an issue and another's perspective of it. In this way, they are more likely to avoid making false assumptions and to be understood by someone else.

Materials required:
- Photocopies of handout 7:1:2 and Six Tips for each individual
- Pens and plain paper
- Whiteboard or paper to record learning

Session plan
1 If the students took part in the three communication games (Exercise 7:1:1), remind them of the frustrations of not being understood.
2 Explain that in this exercise they will be using active listening techniques to make sure that they give other people the opportunity to explain themselves and their issue fully.
3 Give them the handout and read it through with them. Explain with relevant examples as you go along.
4 Ask the students to work in threes and to consider a topic to discuss. Explain that at this stage this should not be a very sensitive issue, just something that one person knows about and would like to discuss.
5 Ask one person to explain the issue and another to use as many of the appropriate questioning techniques as possible. The third person acts as an observer and notes down the different questioning styles.
6 If time permits, let the students change roles.
7 Plenary:
   - How did it feel being listened to like this?
   - How did they feel trying to use the different type of questions?
   - What did they notice as Observer?
   - Which type of questions were most helpful?
   - How might they use this in the future?

Active listening techniques

1 GIVE FULL ATTENTION

- Listen carefully to WHAT is being said.

- Listen carefully to HOW it is being said. Notice the body language.

- Notice what is NOT being said. Can you read anything between the lines?

2 GIVE ENCOURAGEMENT

- Use non-verbal noises — 'Hmmm', 'Oh' — and notice your body language, such as how you are sitting or if you are nodding your head.

- Use helpful supportive statements such as 'Yes I see', and 'I see'.

3 TYPES OF QUESTIONS

- Use **listening questions** : 'Can you give me an example?', 'How did you feel then?' and 'And then what happened?'

- Use **reflective statements**: 'I get the feeling that you are saying...', 'It sounds to me like...'

- Use **summarizing questions**: 'So what you're telling me is...' and 'As I understand it...'

Future Directions © Diane Carrington and Helen Whitten (Network Educational Press, 2005)

Exercise 7:2 Assertive communication

This exercise will help the students to understand what assertive communication is and the benefits of using it in appropriate situations.

Aim To help students understand the advantages of being assertive and the disadvantages of being either passive or aggressive or a mixture of the two.

Benefit Young people will experience many situations where it will be advantageous to be able to express themselves calmly and clearly. It is very useful to understand how to do this in a non-confrontational and appropriate way. This is particularly important when dealing with adults in positions of authority.

Materials required:
- Photocopies of handouts 7:2:1 and 7:2:2 and Six Tips for each individual
- Whiteboard or paper to record learning

Session plan

1 Have a discussion about the difficulties that could be encountered when trying to express your thoughts and opinions. Ask the students for any examples where they felt unable to give their point of view.

2 Ask them what they think aggressive behaviour is (it might help to write the words on the board or on paper). Ask them for a definition and for any examples of aggression they may have experienced, perhaps including being aggressive themselves.

3 Repeat this process to talk about passive behaviour. Then ask the students if there is another way to behave. They might already have heard of assertive behaviour but, if not, prompt them. Ask them to make up their own definition, for example, 'giving mutual respect'.

4 Give them handout 7:2:1 and read through it together, seeing if it agrees with their ideas. Discuss in detail the appropriate use of assertive behaviour, giving examples of where it might not be the correct behaviour to use. You could use the situation in the Story to Share on page 66.

5 Ask the students to get into pairs, give them handout 7:2:2, and ask them to answer the questions. Discuss their answers.

6 If time permits, ask them to think of situations where they would like to be able to act in a more assertive way. They could role-play the situations. Explain the 'broken record' technique of thinking of a reasonable request and repeating it.

7 Plenary:
   - What did they learn about their behaviour?
   - Do adults always act assertively?
   - How can young people handle it when adults don't act in a calm way?
   - Can they think of any situations where it is inappropriate to act assertively?
   - Can they think of any situations where it would help to act assertively?
   - Will they change their behaviour?

Different ways to behave

People don't always display all of these characteristics all of the time, but you might recognize some of these elements in people's behaviour.

Aggressive behaviour

- They get what they want through force, either physical or verbal.
- They don't care about others and often blame them.
- They are out to 'win'.
- Their body language is frightening, finger-pointing, leaning forward.
- They shout and use sarcasm.
- They use words like 'You'd better!', 'You're stupid!', 'You must', 'You should!'

Passive behaviour

- They try to get what they want by making people feel sorry for them.
- They feel like victims and can't stand up for themselves.
- Their body language is crossed arms, hunched shoulders, eyes looking at the floor.
- They have quiet voices.
- They use words like 'I'm useless', 'Maybe', 'It's not important, never mind.'

Passive/aggressive behaviour

- They often appear passive but may suddenly explode into aggression with very little warning.
- They may manipulate people, thinking they will get their revenge later.
- Their body language is often the opposite to what they are saying; they might use sarcasm.
- They use words like 'Perhaps', 'Alright.'

Assertive behaviour

- They try to reach a compromise without damaging others.
- They feel good about themselves and are able to express themselves clearly and calmly.
- Their body language is relaxed, with good eye contact, often smiling!
- They use words like 'I', 'We could', 'What do you think?', How do you feel?'

> **WARNING!!!** THERE MIGHT BE SOME OCCASIONS WHERE IT MIGHT NOT BE APPROPRIATE TO ACT IN AN ASSERTIVE WAY!!!

Future Directions © Diane Carrington and Helen Whitten (Network Educational Press, 2005)

Recognizing different behaviours

Complete the empty boxes. Add some of your own examples overleaf.

	Situation	Response	What type of behaviour is this?	Who gains?	What are the alterna-tive ways of responding?
1	A teacher keeps standing close and staring at a student intimidatingly as he or she works	Student shouts: 'You always pick on me! You're not fair!'	Aggressive	The teacher. The student sent out of the room	
2	A teacher keeps standing close and staring at a student intimidatingly as he or she works	Student ignores teacher Student speaks to the teacher alone after the lesson	Passive Assertive		
3	Mother says to 15-year-old son 'You've got to be in by 10pm tonight'	Boy swears, slams the door and walks out			
4	Teacher gives student detention for no known reason	Student looks down and sighs			
5	A student has put his or her friend's name down to do some extra work	Friend says 'What a nerve! I'm not doing that you idiot!'			
6	A friend fails to turn up as arranged to go out	Friend says 'I suppose it doesn't matter: it was only me who wanted to go anyway'			

Future Directions © Diane Carrington and Helen Whitten (Network Educational Press, 2005)

Exercise 7:3 Peer coaching

Once mastered, this technique could be used by the students to deal with specific individual problems. The exercise is most beneficial if it is undertaken after students have worked on active listening skills in Exercise 7:1:2.

Aim To enable students to understand what coaching is and to practise a simple technique that will enable them to coach their peers.

Benefit Students often ask their friends for advice and this technique will give them the skill to support each other in a mature and useful way.

Materials required:
* Photocopies of handout 7:3 and Six Tips for each individual
* Pens and plain paper
* Whiteboard or paper to record learning

Session plan
1 Explain the benefits of talking over a problem with someone else. Emphasize that this helps to make things clear and logical.
2 Describe the difference between coaching and just chatting. You could use the example of a sports coach, helping someone to achieve his or her full potential. Remind students of the lesson on active listening and the skills required to really listen and understand an issue, as opposed to jumping to wrong conclusions.
3 Give them the handout and read it through together. Make sure they have an understanding of the technique of HELPful coaching.
4 Discuss the type of questions that could be used during the process. If possible, do a role play with a student as an example situation.
5 Ask the students to work in twos: the coach and the coachee. Explain that they should not choose an issue that is too sensitive, but something that the coachee is concerned about and would like to discuss.
6 Give the students ten minutes each to try to use the model to coach each other.
7 Plenary:
   ■ How did they find trying to coach someone?
   ■ How was it different from a usual chat or conversation?
   ■ How did they find being coached?
   ■ Did it help in any way?
   ■ Did it help to make the issues clearer?
   ■ Did it help them to reach any conclusions or plans of action?
   ■ In what situations might coaching someone be helpful?
   ■ Could it help someone who is being bullied?
   ■ Is it a technique that they might use in the future?

HELPful coaching

Remember to use all the active listening skills.

1 HEAR

- First hear what the person wants to talk about.
- Then agree a specific objective of the session.
- Finally, set a long-term goal.

2 EMPATHIZE

- Make sure that you understand what the person is telling you.
- Invite the person to think carefully.
- Make sure you avoid or check any assumptions.
- Ignore anything irrelevant during the discussion.

3 LIST POSSIBLE ACTIONS

- Invite the person to consider as many actions as possible.
- Offer any suggestions carefully and tactfully.
- Try to make sure that choices are made and decisions are reached.

4 PLAN

- Whatever is decided, make sure you agree on a future plan.
- Between you, identify a possible plan of action.
- Make the plans as detailed as possible.
- Decide what support the person might need.

Understanding communication skills

Six Tips

1 If you feel yourself behaving aggressively refer back to the TCP technique practised in Chapter 5.

2 Assertive behaviour allows you to achieve your goals in the short term as well as the long term, so practise it carefully.

3 Body language (how we act and the tone we use) is as important, if not more important, than what we say. Check that yours is appropriate for the message you want to give.

4 Important and formal communication always requires preparation, so give yourself time.

5 Always be very clear yourself what message you want to give and what you want to gain from the communication; this way you will have a much better chance of achieving your goals.

6 We have two ears and one mouth, which should be used in those proportions!

Why bother?

■ You will spend a great deal of your life communicating with others in many different ways. If you practise these techniques you will be able to avoid misunderstandings and manage to understand and to be understood by others.

■ Communication is a complicated process and is often done ineffectively by adults; you will probably have first-hand examples of adults communicating badly themselves. You may have already experienced situations where bad communication led to misunderstandings, which led to more serious repercussions.

■ Many problems develop because of people jumping to the wrong conclusions and these can take time to put right. If you are calm and clear in the first place, it is possible to avoid the upset and to build stable and valuable relationships with others.

My first action step

Commit yourself to one action step over the next week that will help you to understand how communication skills work.

This week I shall:

....

....

....

....

....

....

8 Problem-solving techniques

Our plans miscarry because they have no aim. When a man does not know what harbour he is making for, no wind is the right wind.

SENECA (c4BC–AD65)

Failure is only the opportunity to begin again, this time more wisely.

ANON

YOUR STUDENTS ARE already good at solving problems. They would not have reached this stage of their lives if they had not been able to solve everyday problems such as getting to a friend's house, planning revision, getting themselves on holiday. Most problems can be viewed simply as hurdles that you can overcome using various methods.

The sort of problems students will face in adult life may initially seem more complex than anything they have experienced before. In this chapter we introduce some useful problem-solving techniques that are used successfully by many different individuals and organizations throughout the world. By introducing these techniques to your students at this stage of their lives, you will be equipping them with tools to call upon in many different situations.

The benefits of using techniques to solve problems

There will be many new situations in which students will find themselves for which they are not equipped to deal with successfully. These include:

- being unable to make coursework deadlines;
- having problems with the family;
- deciding what to do in a gap year;
- failing to achieve expected grades;
- failing to get into the college or university of choice;
- being rejected by prospective employers;
- being rejected by friends;
- not being promoted;
- being misunderstood;
- being given too little or too much direction in a first job;
- making mistakes.

What the experts say

Problems aid our self-development because they help us to learn about which methods work and which don't. This is why people often refer to problems as challenges or even learning opportunities. Solving a problem enables you to develop capabilities that you can use in the future to help you manage life. Life is a series of problems and you need to recognize and define what a problem really is before you try to work out a solution. Models have been developed by experts to aid this process, as it has been realized that people need new ways of looking at problems to be able to solve them creatively. Different approaches need to be applied to particular problems, and you must be clear whether you can control, influence or not influence a problem.

An important issue is that of 'problem ownership'. Often, individuals feel that they have to solve every problem that they come across, whether it is their responsibility or not. Transactional analysis – a psychotherapy for personal growth – tells us that often individuals adopt a parent role with their friends and set out to solve all of their friends' problems. The friends then adopt a child role and become dominated and disempowered. It is only by first ascertaining whose problem it really is, that a successful solution can be found, by the right person.

A story to share

Kenji had failed his history A level mock; he was bitterly disappointed, as he felt he had worked hard. His teacher said that she would give him another paper in a month's time to see if he could improve. He decided to sort himself out and really work this time. He decided that he had to learn more dates and facts. He wrote long lists and spent most of his time walking around with the lists repeating them over and over again. When he resat the examination he was amazed to get a similar mark and fail again.

This time he made an appointment to go and see the teacher and discuss his work in detail. Kenji said that he had really worked very hard and he just couldn't understand why he had again got such a low grade. His teacher explained that his work was always too factual, with very little analysis or argument in it. She told him that for A level he must include this analysis to show that he understood what the facts really meant.

Kenji had assumed that he knew what the problem was, without doing any research or checking!

Three steps to solving problems

Each of the following problem-solving exercises can either build on one another or stand alone.

Exercise 8:1 Looking back on past problems

In order to understand how to approach future problems, it can be helpful to consider how you dealt with similar problems in the past. This exercise encourages students to look back and think about what they might have learned. It also requires them to consider if it was really their own problem in the first place, and if getting support or assistance from someone else or somewhere else would have helped.

Because of the requirements of this exercise, some sensitive issues could arise. It might be helpful to be prepared with useful sources of support, such as telephone numbers of organizations or details of websites (see page 191) and a contact person within the school who could offer further support. To avoid any possible embarrassment, it is advisable to display these so that students do not have to request them publicly.

Aim To encourage students to analyse how they dealt with problems in the past and to decide if they have learned anything from this. It also introduces the idea of 'problem ownership'. Finally, the exercise asks them to consider if they might have needed help and, if so, where this might be available.

Benefit In identifying their achievements students will have more confidence in the future when dealing with similar situations.

Materials required:
- Photocopies of handout 8:1 and Six Tips for each individual
- Flip chart, whiteboard or paper to record suggestions
- Lists of relevant support organizations, if required

Session plan
1 Introduce the concept of 'problem ownership'. Explain that seeking help is not a sign of weakness.
2 Ask the students for examples of problems that they have had to deal with in the past. Record their suggestions on the board or paper. Take an appropriate problem and ask: 'Did you really own this problem?'
3 Ask them if there are any problems displayed that might have been solved more easily if the person had got help from somewhere and someone.
4 Give them the handout and ask them to undertake the exercise individually. Point out that you are going to ask them to share their responses with another person, so they should select their problems carefully.
5 Ask them to share their ideas in groups of two or three. Explain that they should be supportive to each other and help to decide whose problem it was, and if any outside help would have been of assistance.
6 Plenary:
    - Did they think that they had developed any useful strategies when dealing with past problems?
    - Had anyone ever tried to solve a problem that did not belong to him or her?
    - Had anyone's comments on a problem and on how he or she had dealt with it been: surprising, helpful, a hindrance?
    - Can we gain any strength from this exercise?

Looking back on past problems

Complete the chart below. Try to think of three problems and give as much detail as possible.

Remember, you are to share this with a partner so choose your problems carefully.

Give details of a problem that you have experienced in the past. Explain how you resolved it.	Do you think that this was really your problem? Did anyone else have any responsibility for it?	Are there any organizations or other people that you could have asked for help to resolve the problem?
1		
2		
3		

Future Directions © Diane Carrington and Helen Whitten (Network Educational Press, 2005)

Exercise 8:2 Using Basadur's Applied Creativity to look at a problem

Basadur's Applied Creativity is a problem-solving technique devised by a Canadian called Dr Min Basadur. Applied creativity encourages people first to define problems and then to come up with creative solutions. This exercise uses one of Basadur's techniques to illustrate to students that it is often essential to work out what the problem really is before they try to solve it.

Aim To give students the opportunity to experience how the technique can help when they are trying to work out what their problems are.

Benefit We often try to solve the wrong problem and nothing improves. By spending time first defining our problems, we make sure that we are dealing with the relevant problem and understand all the aspects of it in detail.

Materials required:
• Photocopies of handout 8:2 and Six Tips for each individual
• Flip chart, whiteboard or paper to record actions

Session plan
1 Introduce Min Basadur's techniques. Explain that Dr Basadur is a leading world expert in the implementation of creative thinking and problem solving, whose processes have helped individuals and organizations all over the world to achieve tangible results. Emphasize that you are going to be using just one of the techniques to help define a problem.

2 Ask the students for possible problems to consider and record their ideas. The technique works best with 'fuzzy' problem areas. Check the questions on the handout first – this will help you to select a problem.

3 Once you have agreed on a problem to consider together, write it at the top of the board or sheet of paper and proceed to ask the questions on the handout. Record some of the students' comments.

4 Explain how this has helped you to gather some information about the problem, which will be useful when deciding if it is the relevant problem to solve.

5 Ask the students to work in groups of four or five. Give them the handouts and explain that they need to undertake the applied creativity process in their groups. It is important to get the groups to agree on a problem quickly. Emphasize that you want to demonstrate the process and technique, which can then be practised at home on real problems.

6. Plenary:
   ■ How did they feel exploring the problem in this way?
   ■ Did they learn anything new about the problem?
   ■ Can they see how this technique could be used to analyse more complex problems?
   ■ Can they think of any problem areas that would benefit from using this technique?

Using Basadur's Applied Creativity to look at a problem

You are going to be using a technique developed by Min Basadur, a Canadian, which he calls 'Fact Finding'. This is taken from his Applied Creativity Problem-solving process.

In your groups, decide on a problem that you can spend time looking at. Try to choose a fairly general problem area.

If possible, write the problem at the top of your paper and ask the questions listed below, or complete this chart. Try to get as much information down as you can. At this stage you are just trying to find out as many facts as possible. Don't discuss the facts in any detail — just write as long a list as possible!

Our fuzzy problem is..

1 What do you know about this situation?

....

....

2 What do you not know about this situation (but would like to know)?

....

....

3 Why is this a problem for you?

....

....

4 What have you already thought of or tried?

....

....

5 If this problem were resolved, what would you have that you don't have now?

....

....

6 What might you be assuming that you don't have to assume?

....

....

Exercise 8:3 Using the Herrmann Thinking Preference Profile to look at a problem

This exercise refers back to the explanation of the Herrmann Thinking Preference Profile (in Chapter 1) to look at a problem from four different viewpoints.

Aim To enable the students to gain a new perspective on a problem.

Benefit Enables your students to become more creative in how they solve problems.

Materials required:
- Photocopies of handout 1:1 (Herrmann's four thinking styles, as used in Chapter 1) and Six Tips for each individual
- Flip chart, whiteboard or paper to record ideas

Session plan
1 Refer to the Herrmann thinking profile in Chapter 1 and remind the students of how people from different quadrants will approach problems from their own perspectives.
2 Ask them for possible problems to consider together, and record their ideas on the board or paper.
3 Once you have agreed on a problem, write it at the top of the board or paper and divide the board into four (following the Herrmann model).
4 Ask the students to work in groups of four or five, and give them the handout defining the quadrants. Ask them how a person from a given quadrant would view the problem. For example, an A quadrant thinker is interested in facts and figures; a C quadrant thinker is interested in 'people' issues. (Remind them to refer to the definitions of the quadrants.) Record some of the students' comments.
5 Explain that they need to undertake the same process in their groups. It is important to get the groups to agree on a problem quickly. Emphasize that you want to demonstrate the process and technique, which can then be practised at home on real individuals' problems.
6 Plenary:
   - How did they feel exploring the problem in this way?
   - Had they learned anything new about the problem?
   - Can they see how this technique could be used to understand how other people view problems?
   - Can they think of any problem areas that would benefit from using this technique?

Problem-solving techniques

Six Tips

1 Recognize and be proud of problems that you have already overcome.

2 Identify what problems you are facing at the moment and consider what methods you could apply to solve them.

3 Always define the positive outcome you would like to happen – don't get stuck in the problem. Unless you know what you want, you won't be taking correct action to achieve it.

4 Make sure it is YOUR problem and not that of someone else. Ask yourself 'Is this problem solvable by me?' If not, try to accept the situation and take a different approach. We can't always solve everything external but we can always choose how we think about it.

5 Ask for help. Often someone else can give you a fresh perspective on how to solve a problem that seems insurmountable to you.

6 You will be solving problems until the day you die, so learn to enjoy them!

Why bother?

- This knowledge and using these techniques will help you to be prepared when problems come your way. Knowing when to challenge something, when to deal with it and when to walk away from it is an important skill.

- Sometimes we become overwhelmed by life's problems and find it difficult to cope. This can happen when we don't have an adequate toolkit of problem-solving techniques, which can make us feel powerless. We find ourselves making comments like: 'Everything I do goes wrong'; 'Just my luck'; 'Life's a bitch'. This results in a victim mentality. By completing this chapter, you have realized that you can take control of problems rather than becoming overwhelmed by them! These tools help you to put your life into perspective and ride the ups and downs without becoming submerged.

My first action step

Commit yourself to one action step over the next week that will help you to develop your problem-solving skills.

This week I shall:

....

....

....

....

....

....

Future Directions © Diane Carrington and Helen Whitten (Network Educational Press, 2005)

9 Unleashing potential

Twenty years from now you will be more disappointed by the things that you didn't do, than by the ones you did do. So throw off the bowlines. Sail away from the safe harbour. Catch the trade winds in your sails. Explore, Dream, Discover!

MARK TWAIN (1835–1910)

DEVELOPING POTENTIAL is fulfilling both for teacher and student. It is not always obvious what a student has to contribute, particularly if he or she is disruptive or appears disinterested. However, as you are aware, pupils all have latent talent that they can choose to develop if they want to and if they receive the encouragement they need.

This chapter will enable students to focus on what they feel like, how they communicate and what they do when they are 'at their best'. It is about peak performance, peak energy and peak contribution – whatever that means to the students themselves.

In our experience, many people have been told at an early age such things as: 'You'll never amount to anything' or 'You won't pass this exam so there is no point taking it' or 'Don't sing in the choir because you are out of tune' or 'You can't paint/draw'. While such an opinion may be valid it is none the less subjective, given by another person with his or her own set of experiences and perspectives. People can hold onto these statements as if they are the 'truth' for the rest of their lives – but they are, in fact, just one person's opinion at a snapshot in time. Young people need to realize that they can take responsibility for their own success beyond the views of teachers and parents, and that if they are to do so they need to work out the science of what it takes for them to be at their best.

Students may have watched some of the *Faking It* programmes on television, where people with no previous experience of a skill such as yacht-racing or playing polo have been able to perform well within four weeks, with the right coaching and encouragement. This programme also demonstrated that it was essential for the person to contribute his or her own energy and persistence to the learning process in order to achieve success. As a young person commented to us recently: 'Watching that programme makes me realize I can achieve anything if I put my mind to it.'

This chapter builds on all that the students have done so far in order to help them make the most of themselves in the adult world.

The benefits of unleashing potential

There can be days when students get out of bed feeling lousy, or other days when they are anxious – for example, when taking an exam, or going for an interview, or starting work for the first time, whether it is a holiday job or a permanent position. Knowing how to make the most of themselves is a lifeskill that enables them to take practical self-help steps whenever they need to. In this way they can operate at peak performance – anytime…anywhere! Some situations when this might be useful are:

- managing an academic or physical challenge;
- life planning;
- career planning;
- rising beyond what and who they have been before;
- sports events;
- acting and music events;
- exams;
- interviews.

What the experts say

Sports psychologists have known for some time how to help people perform and be at their best, how to raise the bar and bring out the potential to achieve greater and greater things. We can learn from them and enable anyone to develop a science of being at his or her best.

Neuro-Linguistic Programming, or NLP, has been described as 'the science of excellence' as it studies role models of excellence in order to understand what makes a person a good mathematician, a good communicator, a good actor, sportsperson or leader. Unwrapping this process and identifying the ingredients of success can enable others to find those elements and qualities within themselves and begin to achieve and be more than they were before. These techniques are now extensively used in business and education as well as in sports and the theatre.

A story to share

John had been ill with glandular fever and had taken nine months off school in the middle of the first year of his A level curriculum. When he came back to school he was anxious about catching up, as he had not done very well in his GCSEs. He was lucky enough to have a wonderful teacher who believed in him and who helped him to create a study and revision plan that resulted in success. John made a time-management plan to cover all his required subjects and wrote down how he needed to feel every day in order to achieve his goals. For example, he took the 'confidence snapshot' [see Exercise 4:3] and chose to feel confident and motivated. He ate healthy food and made time to go for a run in the fresh air every day and to take breaks between periods of study. Using Mind Mapping® and memory techniques for his revision notes and applying positive thinking as he went into his exams, he managed to achieve three A levels at A grades.

Three steps to unleashing potential

These three exercises can be used individually or can build on one another. They are designed to help students identify what it takes on a mental, emotional and practical level for them to be at their best and to develop their potential.

Exercise 9:1 What does it take to be at your best?

In a world where people focus their attention outwards most of the time, we can lose the ability to stop and consider what practical steps we might take to achieve our best.

Aim To help students identify the ingredients of being 'at their best' and what they do to sabotage this.

Benefit Through mental focus and practical steps, students can help themselves to perform at their best in any difficult situation such as an exam, an interview, first week at work, a party.

Materials required:
• Photocopies of handout 9:1 and Six Tips for each individual
• Flip chart, whiteboard or paper to collect ideas
• Magazines (for example, *Hello!*) and scissors

Session plan
1 Introduce the concept of feeling 'at your best'.
2 Show students the magazines and start with a general discussion. Ask them to find photographs of people looking good and looking bad (they should observe what factors influence this – whether it is what they are wearing, facial expression, environmental setting, the fact that they look stressed, or happy – so that they notice the difference). Ask them whether it is external factors – such as clothes – that make people appear to be at their best; or internal factors – such as happiness or confidence – that influence this state.
3 Do factors such as food and drink, life events and adequate sleep affect this for better or worse? Get them to share ideas.
4 Ask them to read the handout and write down their own experiences of what it takes to be at their best.
5 Now get them to share experiences of what it feels like and what influences them – what helps, what hinders this feeling?
6 Ask the students to stand up and show you how they look when they are at their best!
7 Plenary:
   ■ What have they learned?
   ■ How might they apply this technique?
   ■ Could they achieve more if they chose to feel at their best more frequently?

Being at my best

When are you at your best? Think about what influences you, such as clothes, food, sleep, drink, stress, health, mood and relationships. Most of us find that certain situations and certain people bring out the best in us. What brings out the best in you? And what do you do to sabotage your ability to be at your best? Try adding some more examples to the chart below.

What I do to sabotage being at my best	What I need to do to support being at my best
Example: eat too many chips; don't go to the gym; stay up too late	Example: don't go out the night before an interview; eat light food at lunchtime to keep more alert in the afternoon

Make a step-by-step plan that will help you to be at your best when you need to be:

For example: 'I shall get to bed by 11pm'

Step 1: ....

Step 2: ....

Step 3: ....

Step 4: ....

Step 5: ....

Step 6: ....

Future Directions © Diane Carrington and Helen Whitten (Network Educational Press, 2005)

Exercise 9:2 Developing potential

Some young people just do not realize that they have more potential than they may yet have developed. It is possible that their parents are not role models, or that they simply considered certain jobs, skills, strengths and achievements to be unattainable. You can help them to explore possibilities. This exercise is a personal brainstorm to consider what options might lie dormant or what strengths, skills and talents could be built up.

Aim To enable students to explore opportunities to develop their potential.

Benefit Students will gain a broader view of themselves and what is open to them.

Materials required:
- Photocopies of handout 9:2 and Six Tips for each individual
- Pens and plain paper

Session plan

1 Explain that everyone has potential and that although many people start along one road in a career this does not mean that there are not other options open to them.

2 Ask students to imagine that a wizard could give them anything they wanted. What skills, strengths, talents would they like to develop? Tell them not to be modest or doubtful but to believe they could do anything – be a champion footballer, skier, pop star; play an instrument, learn a language; start their own business.

3 Ask them to get into pairs and suggest they think of as many ideas as possible of talents they would like to develop in their lifetimes. Give them five to ten minutes.

4 In their pairs, ask them to assess each talent and decide whether it is realistic; whether it is achievable in the short term or long term.

5 Of their realistic goals, ask them to consider whether they are already beginning to demonstrate any of the skills that may lead to the achievement of this talent. You could give a relevant example such as an actor who began his 'career' in class mimicking a teacher.

6 Plenary:
   - How many ideas were they able to think of?
   - In what way did it help having two brains instead of one?
   - Was it easier to identify someone else's talents rather than their own?
   - What achievable talents did they identify?
   - Were they able to break these down in short- and long-term goals?
   - How will they manage the long-term goals that may take many years to reach?
   - How could they take the first step to achieving one of these?

Developing my potential

With your partner, write down as many ideas as you can of strengths and skills you might like to develop. Don't allow yourself to be limited. The Wizard is there to make your doubts vanish and develop your thinking beyond what you might normally consider.

'If I could do anything I would ...

....

....

....

....

....

....

Exercise 9:3 Mental video visualizing success

This is an exercise to help students build pictures of themselves being successful. It has been proven to aid the achievement of goals.

Aim To bring together all that the students have thought about and identified as goals in Section 1 of this book.

Benefit Visualization has been demonstrated to clarify goals and to help a person to achieve them.

Materials required
- Photocopies of handout 9:3 and Six Tips for each individual
- Your personal 'visualization script' to read from as you lead your students through this exercise

Session plan
1 Explain to the students that they have now been given the opportunity to stop and develop some self-knowledge and build a greater sense of who they are and what they want for themselves in their adult lives.
2 Re-introduce the concept of visualization – which is quite simply building pictures in the mind that crystallize goals and enable individuals to have a better chance of achieving them.
3 Give them the handout and tell them that they can have five minutes to identify the ingredients for their personal visualization. Explain that you will then lead them through this exercise, in which they will picture themselves achieving their goals.
4 When they have completed the first part of the exercise ask them to put down pens and paper. With your 'visualization script' as a guide, talk them through the making of a 'mental video'.
5 Plenary:
   - Did they manage to build some images?
   - Were they actually 'in' the video or were they looking at themselves?
   - How can they plan to use this visualization for themselves as a reminder of their goals and their ability to reach them?

Visualization script for the session leader

This is a suggested script that you can read through as a visualization exercise for the class. You can, of course, alter it according to the needs and level of your students.

Script:
Now that you have started to identify how you might develop your potential and what success might look and feel like, put down your pen and make yourself comfortable.

Shut your eyes and forget about the other people around you. Do not feel embarrassed or worry about what anyone is doing or thinking. This exercise is designed to help you focus on yourself and the achievement of your personal goals. You do not have to share your experience with anyone else and you will not be asked to talk during the visualization. OK, let's go...

Start to build pictures in your mind of becoming successful in some of the goals you have set yourself. This might be learning and mastering a new skill or topic. It might be getting into the university you choose; or being offered the job you wish to have. Equally, it might simply be to feel more confident, energized and capable on a daily basis. Many sports stars have used this type of technique to visualize themselves performing well.

Whatever your goal is, start to build images of yourself walking around the school, feeling more capable of achieving your goals. Build pictures of yourself walking into rooms where you might be meeting teachers, or a prospective boss. You are walking in confident that you have lots of potential and that you are capable of achieving many different goals if you choose to do so. See yourself in as many situations as possible, learning new skills, talking to new people, feeling confident and capable of learning and achieving what you wish to.

As you develop these mental video images of yourself in the future, identify:

- What thought helps you feel at your best? (For example: 'I am a winner' or 'I am going to go for it even if I don't succeed' or 'I might as well give it my all.')
- How does your body feel? Are you standing taller? Are you more relaxed?
- Are you feeling more attractive?
- Imagine yourself more able to express yourself. See yourself as more intelligent.
- What are you saying to those around you?
- How might others know that you are at your best?
- Now have fun and put this video to music. What music helps you feel upbeat? See yourself as more energized, more confident.

Build the pictures, sounds, feelings in your mind. Imagine you really are walking through the school or visiting new places and that in each situation you are feeling more and more confident and able to develop your potential in whatever way you choose. It is a step-by-step process. Imagine yourself over the next few months and start to see and feel yourself being successful.

When you have built some images of the future, realize that you can walk out of this room today feeling like this. Feeling successful comes from inside and you do not have to wait for 'the perfect job' or 'perfect exam result' in order to experience it. The images and the feeling itself will help you to achieve your goals.

Now gradually start to become aware of the room again, to feel your feet on the floor, to hear the sounds of the other people in the room, and when you are ready, open your eyes.

Mental video visualizing success

Identify three of the goals you have made with regard to developing your personal potential and write them below:

1 ....

2 ....

3 ....

Now imagine you are being successful in these endeavours and add words onto each of the branches on the Mind Map® below to capture what success will feel and look like:

What will other people be saying?

What will it look like when you've got there?

How will you be standing, moving, acting?

How will other people know?

How will you be behaving?

Success

What will you be doing?

What will you be saying?

What will it feel like?

Unleashing potential

Six Tips

1 Choose the clothes that make you feel great.

2 Eat food that helps you to feel lively not stodgy or bloated.

3 Skip the alcohol the night before an interview!

4 Get to bed at a reasonable hour so that you feel fully rested – even if you cannot sleep, relax and don't fret about it.

5 Try not to drink too much caffeine as this increases adrenalin and nervousness.

6 Feel successful and you will be more likely to achieve success.

Why bother?

- The Mental Visualization Video is a technique that you can apply to support the achievement of your goals.

- Frequent practice makes it a habit. As Gandhi said, 'Become the change you want to see'.

- We do not know what will happen tomorrow so we might as well enjoy today.

- Being at your best brings out the best in you and is likely to bring out the best in others. When people are feeling good they smile more and other people smile more at them, too.

- Feeling good helps you to stay healthy. You avoid putting stress on your body and your immune system is likely to function better. Being at your best is more likely to make you an attractive and enthusiastic person to work with. This will help you enjoy your work and is likely to lead to positive feedback from your boss or team leader.

My first action step

Commit yourself to one action step over the next week that will help you to unleash your potential.

This week I shall:

....

....

....

....

....

....

....

Section 2

Choices on leaving school

10 Setting goals

Whatever you can do or dream you can, begin it. Boldness has genius, power and magic in it.

JOHANN WOLFGANG VON GOETHE (1749–1832)

U P UNTIL this point most young people's lives will have been shaped by the decisions of parents and teachers; now they need to think for themselves. It is important that they don't feel limited by their past performance or by self-doubts; they need to be encouraged to make a fresh start. This chapter builds on the first section of the book and requires students to think positively about themselves and their future.

According to the principles of Neuro-Linguistic Programming, what you think about is what you create. So encouraging students to consider the limitless possibilities and helping them to plan how to get there will enable them to succeed.

The benefits of setting goals

There are some important moments in young people's lives when they need to make a decision that will have a dramatic impact on their future. These may involve:

- career
- type of work
- study subjects
- personal life
- friends
- activities
- travel.

What the experts say

The brain works automatically 24 hours a day to achieve the goals that you set it. If you don't give it a clear vision of what you want you will find yourself stuck. Research has proven that people who have life goals and write them down are much more likely to achieve them. If you don't know where you are going and have no map it is difficult to get there!

Taking control of our brains and our emotions is now recognized as the most effective way to be successful. The DSE Key Stage Three National Strategy, published in January 2005, states: 'Social, emotional and behavioural skills have been shown to be more influential than cognitive abilities for personal and academic success.' Therefore adopting the right attitude will enable students to be confident when they plan for the future.

It is also acknowledged that it is necessary to help students to break their visions of the future down into manageable stages. In this way they will be able to plan each step towards reaching their ideal life situation.

A story to share

A couple had a little boy, who they called Bert. As a baby he didn't learn to talk. Whatever they tried they couldn't get him to say anything. They took him to their doctor, who suggested they just wait and see what happened in the future. Bert finally started to talk when he was about four years old. He used to have tantrums and get into terrible moods, and when he went to school he was often in trouble. Teachers complained to his parents that he was always daydreaming and did not join in with the other children.

Because his father's business was going badly, Bert's family had to move several times and eventually they decided to try again in a different country. By this time Bert was 15 and as he seemed to have settled down a bit his parents left him at boarding school – but he hated it. According to some opinions, he was expelled, although others say that he pretended to be ill so that he could leave. One day, to his parents' surprise, he just turned up at their new home. They were worried about his future and because he didn't have a good report he couldn't get into the best college.

However, when he grew up he became one of the most famous scientists that ever lived, winning the Nobel Prize for Physics in 1921. He was Albert Einstein.

Three steps to setting goals
Each of the following three exercises can either build on the others or stand alone.

Exercise 10:1 Life timeline

In order to set positive goals for themselves, it is important for students to reflect on their past; to acknowledge the highs and lows and to recognize their achievements. In this exercise they look back over their lives and make a note of the important times. Encourage them to be honest. Explain that every life is made up of good and bad times, and that it is possible to move on. Remind them that if we learn from a situation it makes us stronger and more able to deal with problems in the future.

Aim To help students recognize the effect that events in their lives have had on them. They need to accept what has happened to them so far and move on. Individuals might need support if they have had many negative experiences.

Benefit Enables students to come to terms with difficult situations and to build on positive ones.

Materials required:
• Photocopy of Six Tips for each individual
• Flip chart, whiteboard or paper to record ideas and actions

Session plan

1 Introduce the importance of accepting who we are.

2 Give some examples of successful people who have conquered adversity.

3 Discuss the skill of learning lessons from negative situations and becoming stronger because of them.

4 Give each student a blank piece of paper and ask him or her to draw a timeline from their birth to the present day. You could draw an example on the board.

5 Ask them to work in twos and threes and discuss their timelines. Explain that they should support each other in trying to find out what they could have learned from each situation and event.

6 Plenary:

   ■ What has been learned and what strengths have you gained?

   ■ How might they use this knowledge in the future?

   ■ How can they focus on the positive events?

Exercise 10:2 Prioritizing

This exercise will help students to decide what are the most important things they want from life.

Aim To help students decide what options they have, in order to work out where they want to go.

Benefit Recognizing that sometimes we have to compromise some of our wants in order to achieve our most important goals.

Materials required:
• Photocopies of handout 10:2 and Six Tips for each individual
• Flip chart, whiteboard or paper to record learning points

Session plan

1 Introduce the concept of prioritizing what is most important. Explain that this list will change as we develop, due to growing older, the situation we find ourselves in and the people that we meet.

2 Pick a couple of statements from the handout and ask the students what is most important to them. For example: who wants to work mainly inside or who wants to work mainly outside?

3 Explain that you want to record a snapshot of their current priorities for the future.

4 Give them the list of statements and ask them to individually tick the ones that apply to them. Then ask them to select the five statements that are most important to them and to number them from 1 to 5, from the most important to the least important.

5 Ask them to work in twos and threes and compare their lists. Encourage them to explain the reasons for their choices.

6 Plenary:

   ■ How did they feel sharing their lists of priorities?

   ■ What did they find out about their partners?

   ■ Do they think they will always have the same priorities? If not what will change them?

   ■ How might it help them to know what is most important to them?

Possible priorities

Tick the statements that apply to you.

Select the five statements most important to you and number them in order of importance from 1 to 5.

❑ I want to work outside

❑ I want to work inside

❑ I want to work with other people

❑ I want to work alone

❑ I want to find out about lots of different things

❑ I want to earn lots of money

❑ I want to do good for other people

❑ I don't care so much about money as long as I enjoy my work

❑ I don't want to work at weekends or evenings

❑ I want to use my own initiative

❑ I want to have a family

❑ I want to have pets

❑ I want time to pursue my hobbies

❑ I want to travel abroad

❑ I want to live abroad

❑ I want to go to college

❑ I want to live away from home at college

❑ I want to live at home while at college

❑ I want to get married

❑ I want to be famous

❑ I want to care for others

Exercise 10:3 Visualizing your perfect life situation

It is often difficult to be specific and detailed about our goals. This exercise asks each of your students to storyboard his or her perfect life.

Aim To help the students to visualize what their perfect life situations would look like, so that they will know in detail where they want to go.

Benefit By defining exactly what they are aiming for they will be able to plan in detail how they can get there.

Materials required:
- Sheet of A3 plain paper for each individual
- Flip chart, whiteboard or paper to collect ideas

Session plan
1 Explain how visualizing a situation allows you to break down the route to get there into manageable steps.
2 Explain that they should try to be as detailed as possible with their visualization. They can refer to Exercise 10:2 on priorities, if they have already completed this.
3 Explain that you want them to storyboard their perfect life situations. Emphasize that this isn't an art lesson and that it is acceptable to draw symbols to represent objects. You could draw some examples on the board – a stick person, a smiley face, a tree to represent the countryside.
4 Give out the A3 paper and ask them to draw a storyboard. Allow them 15 minutes to complete it. Explain that they should start at the end with the perfect situation and work backwards, depicting how they got there (at college, at work, meeting people and so on).
5 Ask them to share their storyboards in pairs. They should explain what the drawings represent.
6 Plenary:
   - How did it feel deciding what to include?
   - Were they surprised at their partner's visualizations?
   - How could they use these storyboards to make decisions about their future?

Setting goals

Six Tips

1 Recognize the positive things you have gained from your life so far (even negative experiences have taught you valuable lessons).

2 Be aware of what is important to you; this will help you to focus on it and to ultimately achieve it.

3 Remember, your brain likes to have a goal so it knows what to aim for.

4 Don't set your goals too high in the beginning. 'The way to eat an elephant is in bite-size pieces'; make each step achievable in the near future.

5 Give yourself milestones along the way – little rewards help to motivate us.

6 Don't let little setbacks put you off, things never go 100 per cent as planned.

Why bother?

■ Whether or not you decide to take control of your life it is certain that by this time next month, or next year, things will be different. You can just let things happen to you or you can take positive steps to have some influence on what happens.

■ You are capable of achieving whatever you want if you are prepared to work for it. This might take time and great effort, but amazing things are possible. As soon as you start to believe in yourself and your capabilities, you will act differently and others will start to believe in you.

■ People with extraordinary disadvantages have managed to overcome them and make incredible achievements in life. This demonstrates that your own determination and self-belief can put you, too, on the fast track to achieving the lifestyle you want. Learning to break this vision down into manageable steps is a skill that will enable you to manage your everyday tasks and projects for the rest of your life – and even achieve your dreams!

My first action step

Commit yourself to one action step over the next week that will help you to set goals.

This week I shall:

....

....

....

....

....

....

....

11 To college or not to college?

The direction in which education starts a man will determine his future life.
PLATO (427–347BC)

ALL STUDENTS have to decide whether they should go to college immediately, in the future or perhaps never. There are a wide variety of options available to them and they will need support and information while making this important decision. There are many different factors that will affect their decision and many of these have been covered earlier in this book. Students need to consider the qualifications their chosen career requires, as well as the social and economic factors, such as the cost of going to college and what their friends will be doing.

The exercises in this chapter cover many of the most important considerations. You should remind students of the decisions about their futures they have already made – for example, what lifestyle and values they would like to achieve. It is easy to decide to go to college for the wrong reasons, because of parental or school or peer group pressure. It is important to emphasize that they are likely to be at college on their own, away from people who might have influenced their decision, so it is imperative that where they end up is their own choice.

The benefits of taking time to decide

Each of the options available to students will have its own benefits and these include:

Going to college immediately:
- No break in study might be easier.
- It gives the opportunity to mature, especially if the college is away from home.
- Qualifications still lead to jobs with higher salaries.
- College time is enjoyable.
- It gives the opportunity to meet new people.

Taking a gap year:
- It gives the possibility to travel.
- It gives the opportunity to become more self-reliant.
- Some professions like examples of independent problem solving.
- It might offer the chance to earn some money.

- It gives the opportunity to meet new people from different cultures.
- It can be very enjoyable and rewarding.

Undertaking a part-time course:
- It is possible to get sponsored posts that will guarantee a job.
- It gives the opportunity to earn money while you are studying.
- A vocational course avoids studying subjects that might lead nowhere.
- It gives the opportunity to meet new people involved in the work you want to do.
- It gives you the opportunity to keep up with friends at home.

Never going to college in the foreseeable future:
- Work suits some people better than college.
- Many jobs still offer the possibility to work up from the shop floor.
- Valuable hands-on experience can be gained.
- It is possible to earn money immediately.
- It gives the opportunity to meet new people involved in the work you want to do.

What the experts say

The decision that students make now will have an immediate and dramatic effect on their lives. It is recognized that often young people find it very daunting committing themselves to long, possibly arduous, college courses. Three years or even more can sound like a lifetime to 17 year olds. Students often equate college with school and feel that they will be treated by lecturers in the same way as they are treated by teachers. Many university courses now have only four or five hours of lectures per week, with tutorials once a month, which is very different from the pastoral care received by students at school. It can be very beneficial to get some young people already undertaking similar courses to come into school to tell your students what it is really like, both the work demands and the social life. These college students can be your up-to-date experts.

Although it is necessary to stress the importance of this decision it is also essential to help the students realize that it is very common for people to return to studying throughout their lives as they shift their own personal focus and as the job market changes – and the changes have been dramatic over the past few years. People very rarely have a job for life and the 'zigzag' career has emerged, with people taking transferable skills from one job to the next.

There has been much research on the cost of going to college, especially with rises in student tuition fees. In a MORI survey in 1999, Madsen Pirie and Robert Worcester found that university students spend more on drink and entertainment than on tuition fees, and twice as much on clothes as on books. They also found that students think that their investment in education will help them to get good jobs in the future. It is clear that there are many benefits, both social and educational, in going to college.

It is also essential to emphasize that whatever college or university course young people decide to undertake they will learn and develop, and gain many of these transferable skills that will be very useful to them throughout their lives, even if they decide to change direction in the future. No learning is ever a waste of time!

A story to share

Ivan was eager to go to university; both his brothers had been a few years earlier and had told him what an amazing time they had there. When he first arrived, it didn't surprise Ivan that he was nervous. He always felt awkward meeting new people but he resolved to make greater efforts. He went along to the Freshers' Fair and joined four different societies. Unfortunately, two of them didn't get going. When he went to the other two they seemed to be made up of second and third year students, who all knew each other.

Ivan didn't have much more luck with his lectures. They were attended by an enormous number of students and he never managed to sit next to the same person twice in the first few weeks.

Like many other students in the first year, he was unable to get into the university halls of residence on campus and he lived in a very dilapidated flat with two other students. One of his flatmates was a mature student, who went home every weekend, and the other boy had very different interests from Ivan – for example, they liked completely opposite kinds of music – and as Ivan was reading English and the other boy was reading physics their studies didn't give them much in common.

Ivan was miserable. He spent most of his time in the library, or in his flat reading. He just couldn't see a way out. Finally, when he went home during reading week, he decided he didn't want to go back. He loved the subject, but was very unhappy at the college.

One year later, after many visits to college open days and staying with friends at their universities for the weekend, Ivan started at a different university. This one he loved – it was just as social and exciting as he had hoped. Three years later he graduated with a 2:1 degree.

Three steps to helping you decide whether or not to go to college

Each of the following exercises has been designed to encourage students to take time and consider all the options open to them at this decision-making stage of their lives.

Exercise 11:1 Undertaking in-depth web-based research

This exercise requires access to a computer. As a research tool the internet can be very useful but, without guidelines, trying to find a piece of information or the answer to a particular problem can be frustrating and time-wasting.

Aim To help students find out about different types of colleges, by undertaking web-based research.

Benefits Not only will the students find out about the opportunities offered by the colleges, but they will also practise a useful technique of how to search efficiently on the web.

Materials required:
• Photocopies of handout 11:1 and Six Tips for each individual
• Pens and paper
• Whiteboard or paper to record learning
• PCs with access to the internet

Session plan
1 Introduce working on the internet. The web offers access to millions of sites that could provide vital information and, even more useful, the ability to search these sites within a relatively short period of time. However, it is important to give the students objectives so that they don't get sidetracked. Both colleges and business organizations often have detailed websites that can be obtained from a search engine.

2 It is best if the students work alone, but it is possible for them to work in pairs if they share similar interests.

3 Give them the handout and explain that they have a limited time to complete the questions. Emphasize that they should not get sidetracked into irrelevant details.

4 Plenary:

    After the research it is beneficial to conduct some feedback in a discussion so that the students can share their findings. Ask them:

    ■ What was the most interesting or surprising thing you found out?
    ■ Was it easier or more difficult than you imagined?
    ■ Was there anything it was impossible to find out?
    ■ What was the most interesting website?
    ■ Have you changed any of your ideas about the future?

To college or not? Web-based research

It is important to work through these questions in order. Try not to become sidetracked!

1 What career or job are you considering?

....

....

2 Do you know what qualifications are required for these careers or jobs? If you don't know the requirements, try to find them out and record them here:

....

....

3 How would you go about gaining these qualifications?

☐ FE college?

☐ University?

☐ Specialist college?

4 Visit the college websites and try to answer the following questions:

- What is the title of the course offered?
- What are the academic requirements to get on the course?
- How many students are on the course?
- What are the titles of the units constituting the course?
- How is the course examined (written, coursework)?
- Where do the majority of first-year students live?
- When are the open days?
- What societies would you consider joining?

Exercise 11:2 Two case studies to consider

Although paper based and able to be undertaken individually, this exercise can also be undertaken in groups as the students will benefit from discussing the choices made by the two characters in the case studies. The examples illustrate that there is often more than one route into a career.

Aim To ask the students to consider the best route into a career.

Benefit Highlights the pros and cons of alternative routes, which will have consequences for lifestyle and earning power.

Materials required:
• Photocopies of handout 11:2 and Six Tips for each individual
• Pens and paper

Session plan
1 Give the students the two case studies to read and to answer questions on.
2 It is possible for the students to either work alone on the questions or to work in pairs or in small groups. If they collaborate, they could consider their answers and present them to the other participants for a general discussion.
3 Give time for the groups to present their answers to the class.
4 Plenary:
   ■ Were the end results very different?
   ■ Were there any facts in the stories that you found surprising?
   ■ How do people make decisions about their routes into their jobs?
   ■ What can you learn and take forward for yourself from these stories?

Two case studies to consider

Case Study A

John left school at 15, desperate to get to work and earn some money. He joined an insurance company, where his tasks were to collect the mail in the morning, get tea and coffee when required and to do photocopying for the underwriter he sat next to. John did this for three years, when he at last managed to get promotion to office admin assistant. He still had to do the photocopying but he also got to do the filing and opening the letters, which someone else delivered to him. After another two years, now aged 20, he decided to take the insurance exams, which would enable him to gain more promotion. These exams took him four years, during which time he got to know the business and the brokers and clients. He finally became an assistant underwriter after nine years with the company and an underwriter three years later.

By the time John was 50, he was a partner in the company and earning over £100,000 a year.

Case Study B

Kay did her A levels at school and went on to university to study economics. After her three-year degree, at the age of 21, she went into a large insurance company as a trainee graduate. It was a two-year programme which she often found boring. The company sent her to Toronto for six months, where she felt lonely, and she was pleased to get back to her friends.

Kay then changed jobs and moved to another insurance company in Lloyd's, where she started off as an office administrator. After a year, she became an assistant underwriter and started to take her insurance exams, which took her another two years.

By the time Kay was 50, she was a partner in the company and earning over £100,000 a year.

Questions:

1 Which route would you prefer into this job?

2 What would John and Kay's lives have been like during their early years up until the age of 21?

3 What different experiences would they have had?

4 What are the advantages of each route?

5 What are the disadvantages of each route?

6 What different skills would they each bring with them?

7 What affected their decisions?

8 Did anything surprise you about these case studies? They are both true.

Future Directions © Diane Carrington and Helen Whitten (Network Educational Press, 2005)

Exercise 11:3 The pros and cons of going to college – a classroom debate

Often, students themselves are aware of the pros and cons of decisions they have to make. This exercise requires them to present their ideas in a structured and coherent way. It will help them to clarify what they need to consider when making a decision. Although this exercise does work as a stand-alone, it is particularly powerful when completed after Exercise 11:1 or 11:2, as the students can use either their own research or the case studies as evidence.

Session plan

1 The class should be divided into two groups. One group is to speak for going to college and the other group is to speak against going to college. (If working on a one-to-one basis or in a small group, two individuals can put the opposing views.)

2 Suggested format for the debate:

- Each group should provide three speakers who will each give a five-minute talk from their given perspective.

- Groups will be given ten minutes to prepare their case.

- After each talk, the other side will have five minutes to question the speaker. The rest of the group will be able to assist the speaker in answering the questions.

- After all the talks and questions the subject is open to the floor for a general debate chaired by the teacher.

To college or not to college?

Six Tips

1 Make sure you take time to consider what career you would like to do and carefully research all the possible routes into it.

2 Speak to as many people as possible that have relevant experience, as first-hand knowledge is invaluable.

3 Don't be afraid to ask for help – there are many organizations, such as the Connexions service, which are there to help you. They have a confidential drop-in service, which you can go to without anyone else knowing.

4 Many colleges and universities have open days, which they advertise well in advance on their websites. Make a note of any you are considering and go along. Open days include guided walks around the college and talks giving you information about college life.

5 Read biographies of people who you admire, to find out how they succeeded. You will be surprised by how many didn't follow the traditional college route into their jobs.

6 Remember the final decision is yours, so make sure you choose what you really want to do, and not just what is expected of you. This is your chance to start something exciting and new!

Why bother?

When you are considering your future you should remember that it is your first step into adult life and whatever you choose will have serious repercussions. By taking time now to consider all the possibilities and opportunities open to you, you will have less chance of getting it wrong. Although it is important to remember that it is alright to 'get it wrong' – as all life experiences make us stronger and more able to deal with problems in the future – it is better and easier to get it right the first time.

My first action step

Commit yourself to one action step over the next week that will help you to consider whether to go to college now, in the future or never.

This week I shall:

....

....

....

....

....

....

....

12 Work possibilities

Choose a job you love, and you will never have to work a day in your life.

CONFUCIUS (C551–478 BC)

OVER THE PAST few years there have been many changes in the world of work. Each day, jobs are being taken over by technology and new ones are being created. Not only are the contents of jobs changing, but also the way in which they are being undertaken: home working, virtual teams and many organizations functioning 24/7 have changed the nature of work.

With the rise in vocational education and courses, and the development of modern apprentices, there are more choices than ever available to young people. In making decisions about work, many factors have to be considered such as lifestyle, goals, values and personality fit. Many of these areas have been developed earlier in this book and it will be beneficial to students to complete some of the previous chapters before undertaking this one.

The benefits of considering all work possibilities

Decisions about what work to aim for are complicated and complex. If students make the wrong decisions it can lead to a difficult start for them. Applying for jobs is not only time-consuming but also stressful. If one is attending an interview unprepared it can lead to a reduction in one's self-esteem and confidence that can take time to repair. Careful research and planning not only saves time, but can also result in a better prepared and more confident candidate.

Some of the reasons why it is important to consider carefully all work possibilities are:

- to make as close a fit as possible with qualifications and characteristics;
- to avoid missing opportunities that parents and teachers are unaware of;
- to understand exactly what different jobs entail;
- to make it less likely that students miss an ideal job.

What the experts say

Because of the improvements in communications, not only are there many new jobs but people are also often working in different ways. In 2004, the Office of National Statistics (ONS) found that more than 2.1 million people worked from home and 8 million spent at least some of their working week in the house. Experts predict 5 million of us will be working from home by 2007. DTI figures show that among employees who requested flexible working, 77 per cent were fully accepted by employers and in 9 per cent of cases a compromise was reached. This new flexible way of working will obviously affect many individuals.

The development of the 'zigzag' career is quite recent. This is when people no longer change their jobs within the same career field but retrain and relaunch themselves into a new, divergent career. Not only are people likely to make changes because of family or health considerations, but also because their jobs change due to developments in technology. Therefore the knowledge that they gain about the various opportunities in work will be invaluable throughout their lives.

These recent developments mean that it is imperative that students undertake thorough research into all the latest possibilities. This time will not be wasted, as even after they have decided on a job the chances are that they will change careers quite dramatically during their working lives.

There are also numerous new courses such as the Vocational and Applied A levels and GCSEs, which offer close links with work and will give students the opportunity to research careers while still at school. There are also many ways into work such as the Apprentice Scheme, which can be researched on the DfES and Connexions websites.

A story to share

Sam didn't really like much at school apart from information technology, which he enjoyed and was good at. His reports were never satisfactory, except in that one subject. He spent every spare minute around horses – they were his passion. He didn't have his own horse but a friend sometimes let him ride his horse.

Sam lived near a large racetrack and loved to watch the horses training early in the morning. Sometimes his dad would take him to the races and would place bets on Sam's favourite horses.

When Sam was about to leave school his parents were worried that he would never find a decent job. Most of his friends had decided to go to college or on an apprentice scheme, but Sam wasn't interested. One day he saw an advertisement for someone who was good at IT and interested in horses to work in a large stables that ordered feedstuff, planned riding lessons and logged their invoices on the computer. Sam couldn't believe his luck. He applied immediately and surprised them at the interview with his immense knowledge of both IT and horses. He got the job!

Three steps to considering work possibilities

The exercises in this chapter have been designed to encourage students to consider the wide range of work possibilities available to them, before they make their choice.

Exercise 12:1 A work review

Although this review needs to be undertaken alone, it is useful to allow time for a group discussion to see if there are any common trends and feelings about different types of work.

Aim To encourage students to think about all the different types of work they have done already and to recognize the skills they have developed.

Benefit Often young people find it hard to appreciate that every job involves transferable skills, which they can use in other jobs. This exercise will help them to identify the skills they have already obtained.

Materials required:
• Photocopies of handout 12:1 and Six Tips for each individual
• Whiteboard or paper for recording learning

Session plan
1 Discuss with the students what type of work they have already undertaken. They will probably need some prompting, as they will often only consider work to be jobs they have been paid for; also, they might not immediately see the skills involved in the menial tasks they have performed.
2 It would therefore be helpful to pick an example relevant to the level of the group, such as babysitting, working as a cashier in a supermarket or helping in a cafe, and list all the skills required for the job on the board or on paper at the beginning of the lesson.

Examples:

Babysitter
   ■ Honest – *Alone in the house with private belongings*
   ■ Reliable – *Must arrive on time and not leave until adults return*
   ■ Competent – *Able to analyse a situation and alert adults if necessary*
   ■ Good child-handling skills – *Able to get the children to behave and go to bed*

Cafe staff
   ■ Honest – *Handling money*
   ■ Reliable – *Must arrive on time and stay as long as required*
   ■ Good customer-handling skills – *Some customers are difficult to deal with*
   ■ Good at maths –*Able to give correct change*

3 Give the students the handout and ask them to complete it individually.
4 Ask them to share their responses in pairs, in groups, or with the whole class.
5 As they are likely to put down similar types of jobs, it would be useful to compare the skills required to see who has the longest and most comprehensive list.
6 Plenary:
   ■ Was there anything surprising on your list?
   ■ Did you have more skills than you expected?
   ■ What does this say about you?
   ■ How might you be able to use this knowledge when you write your CV or go to a job interview?

Transferable skills chart

Complete the chart below with as much detail as possible.
Continue on the back of the sheet if necessary.

Type of job: this can be paid or voluntary (eg babysitting, shop assistant etc)	How many hours a week did this job take?	What skills did you use in this job? (list as many as possible)	What did you enjoy about the job?	What did you dislike about the job?	Can you think of any other similar jobs?
1					
2					
3					
4					
5					

Exercise 12:2 Detailed photo reading

This exercise allows students to use their powers of deduction to see how many jobs there are displayed in a photograph. It encourages them to think about the wide variety of jobs that might be available in their immediate surroundings.

Aim To encourage students to appreciate the range of jobs available.

Benefit It is easy to underestimate the jobs that are available and this will highlight both the wide diversity of jobs and encourage the students to think of jobs in 'families'.

Materials required:
- Photocopies of handout 12:2 (see *www.networkpress.co.uk/resources* for colour version) and Six Tips for each individual
- Flip chart, whiteboard or paper to record the ideas

Session plan
1 Introduce the idea that there are more jobs available than they might have previously considered.
2 Give students the handout and read through the example of the water bottle. Use this to make it clear how detailed you want them to be. Ask the students to work in groups of three or four and make a list of all of the jobs involved in creating the scene. Give them ten minutes and remind them to number their ideas.
3 Ask each group to tell you how many jobs they managed to find. Listen to some examples.
4 Introduce the idea of 'job families'. You could follow the system currently used in your school's careers information or write headings on the board or on paper, for example: computers and technology; business and finance; environment and conservation; engineering and mechanical; arts and entertainment; transportation and tourism; manufacturing and retail; construction; science. Ask the students to put each job they have identified into the correct family and see if they can generate more jobs.
5 Ask the students to count up how many jobs they found in each 'job family'. Compare the totals.
6. Plenary:
   - Were there more jobs visible than you had imagined?
   - What was the most commonly found 'job family'?
   - Did this surprise you?
   - Usually the most commonly found family is manufacturing. Was this what you found and, if so, why do you think this is?
   - What does this tell us about the nature of jobs?
   - What does this tell us about the world of work?

Detailed photo reading

Study the picture below and list the jobs that have been involved to produce what is shown. For example, the bottle of water on the ground in the bottom left-hand corner involved:

• people making the clear plastic for the bottle

• people designing the label for the bottle

• people printing the label

• people producing the water

• people marketing the bottle

• people selling the bottle.

Photo: Diane Carrington

Exercise 12:3 A research project

This project will inevitably take place predominantly outside school, apart from the web-based research, and so is ideal for homework. It uses some of the same research tactics explained in Exercise 11:1 for looking at college websites, and could follow on from that exercise.

Aim To give the students the opportunity to research careers in which they are particularly interested.

Benefit It is easy to be vague when choosing a job and this exercise will give them the skills to undertake personal research to find out all the details they need.

Materials required:
• Photocopies of handout 12:3 and Six Tips for each individual
• For the web-based research, computers and access to the internet

Session plan
1 Explain why it is important to undertake careful research into different jobs. This is useful both before you start looking and if you are offered a job and don't know what it entails.
2 Explain that you want students to choose a job or a profession that they are seriously considering.
3 Give them the research guide handout and let them work on the computers. Although this is ideally undertaken alone, it is possible to put students into groups of two or three who are interested in the same job area. Ask them to undertake some research and try to find out some answers to the questions on the handout. Allow them 20 minutes.
4 Ask the students how many questions they managed to answer and for how many jobs.
5 For homework, ask them to interview someone about his or her job and find out as much as possible about it.
6 Plenary:
   ■ Did they find it easy or difficult to find information?
   ■ Did anything surprise them about their findings?
   ■ Has the research made anyone change his or her mind about what job he or she would like?
   ■ Did they find out anything different in their interviews?
   ■ Did they find out anything surprising in the interviews?
   ■ How might these skills be useful in the future?

Research project

Name: ....

Class: ....

Complete as much of this questionnaire as possible.

1 What job or career are you considering?

....

2 What are the entrance qualifications for this job or career?

....

3 What are the names of some of the companies involved in this work?

....

4 From their website, answer the following questions about the company you are researching:

a) What is the name of the company? ....

b) How many people do they employ? ....

c) Where are their offices? ....

d) What is the main nature of their work? ....

e) When were they founded? ....

f) Do they have any recent press releases? If so, what are they about?

....

....

g) What else seems important about this organization?

....

....

Try to answer questions (a)–(g) for as many companies as possible.

Future Directions © Diane Carrington and Helen Whitten (Network Educational Press, 2005)

Work possibilities

Six Tips

1 Make sure you are fully aware of the transferable skills you already have from part-time jobs or voluntary work.

2 Try to become aware of all of the different jobs that exist around you. If you have a hobby or an interest, try to find out what jobs are connected to it.

3 Use the internet to research any interests that you have, to find out what jobs are involved in that area.

4 When you find a job that you are considering, try to talk to people who already do a similar job and ask them how they entered the profession.

5 Check that you are aware of all the new courses available which will give you experience of work, such as Vocational and Applied GCSEs and A levels.

6 Find out what apprentice schemes are available to you in your chosen field. There are many organizations that will be able to give you this information, such as the Connexions service.

Why bother?

■ Many people just stumble into work and realize after a few weeks, or unfortunately after a few years, that they don't actually like their job. They claim 'I just sort of ended up here!'.

■ When you consider how long people are in work, and with the next generation probably working until they are in their 80s, it is tragic that so many people end up doing something that they don't enjoy. By starting off with careful, thorough research you are more likely to end up in a job you enjoy and that uses your skills and talents as well as paying the rent!

My first action step

Commit yourself to one action step over the next week that will help you to find out what jobs are available in areas that interest you.

This week I shall:

....

....

....

....

....

....

....

13 Preparing for interviews and meeting people

It usually takes more than three weeks to prepare a good impromptu speech.
MARK TWAIN (1835–1910)

YOUR STUDENTS MAY not be used to stating their strengths, talents or aspirations, but they must be prepared to do so when they go for an interview or meet new people. There is always great competition for jobs and college places and they must learn to present themselves as positively and confidently as possible. You need to help students to realize that they have only one chance to make a first impression and that to do this they have to plan carefully. They need to demonstrate their 'Wow' factor that will make an interviewer sit up and listen.

This chapter gives you the information, the tools and the techniques to help to empower your students. It builds on Chapters 1 and 2, where the students explored their strengths and talents.

The chapter also refers to the 'elevator pitch', and encourages them to use this technique in as many situations as possible. It is important to remind them that the more they practise this technique, the more comfortable they will become using it and the more natural and believable they will sound both to themselves and others.

The benefits of preparing for interviews and meetings

There are some important occasions where young people will have to express themselves in a confident, positive way in order to achieve their goals. These include:

- where there is competition for places;
- when they want to stand out from the crowd;
- when they want to demonstrate what they have to offer: their personal skills and qualities;
- when they want to fit into an environment or culture;
- when they need to raise their profile, or to get others to take them more seriously.

What the experts say

Body language is very important in giving away what we really mean; 93 per cent of what you say is how you say it and only 3 per cent is what you actually say. Body language also includes the tone of your voice and your speech patterns. This means that it is essential to make sure that there is consistency with all of our body language. Experts talk of 'non-verbal leakage', when signs are displayed by our bodies that are in opposition to what is actually being said. These signs include lack of eye contact, fidgeting and putting hands over your mouth. Call centres have techniques to check if callers are telling the truth by the way they phrase their sentences and even by the way they breathe.

Our bodies are physiologically designed to make quick decisions; we are capable of deciding instantly if someone is a friend or foe. Interviewers often use this same technique when they are faced by several candidates with similar qualifications; they go with their 'gut reaction'. They often decide on the person who appears to fit in with their existing culture.

The media also rely on people making quick decisions. In advertising, very short television adverts contain many symbols of the supposedly desired lifestyle, which the customer is expected to aspire to. Audiences have been shown to recognize such symbols and identify with them immediately, which encourages them to purchase the product. In the 1970s subliminal projection was used by advertising agencies, where an image was flashed on the television screen for a split second – so briefly that the audience did not consciously 'see' it. Tests showed that after watching the advertisement the majority of people identified the projected object. This technique was thought to be dangerous and was made illegal for use by advertisers.

Makers of TV soap operas also use stereotypes, people who can be identified by an audience in a split second. Politicians recognize the power of being judged by how they say things, and so they employ image consultants to plan what to say, how to say it and what to wear while they are saying it. With the rise of media literacy it is not surprising that we are now constantly reading visual signs and signifiers and making very quick decisions.

A story to share

Carmel and Alex were both candidates for the same job as a research assistant in a pharmaceutical company. Both of them felt that the interview had been a disaster.

Alex had failed to find out more about what the company did. When the interviewer asked him what he thought he could bring to the job, Alex spoke about his friendly, chatty personality and said that he liked to be actively involved with exciting projects. The interviewer had looked at him with disdain and explained that the research assistants worked in an almost silent laboratory, undertaking research of competitors' websites.

Carmel's interview didn't go any better. She forgot to mention on her CV or at the interview that she had once had a summer holiday job at a pharmaceutical company. Her nerves got to her and she just talked endless rubbish about working in a nursery.

Continued

When both candidates received a letter telling them that they hadn't got the job they were naturally disappointed, but reacted very differently. Alex's thoughts were:

'I knew I was rubbish! I always mess up interviews, I hate them. I shouldn't have applied for this job, I'm obviously not up to it. I'll never get a decent job, I don't know why I bother.'

Carmel's thoughts were:

'I can't believe I didn't tell them about my experience in a similar company! Goodness knows what came over me. I must remember to make sure that I always manage to get in all the relevant information in the future. Next time, I'll make a note of what I think they want and I'll make sure that I mention any relevant or similar experience. If it doesn't come out in the interview, perhaps I could think of a question to ask the interviewer at the end that gives me the opportunity to tell them what I've done. I could say something like, "What are the lunch arrangements here, as when I was working at another pharmaceutical company a sandwich lady came round". I wonder where else I can apply?'

How do you think the candidates' thoughts will affect their future?

Three steps to preparing for interviews and meeting people

Each of the three following exercises can either build on the others or stand alone.

Exercise 13:1 First impressions: body language and stereotyping

Learning to read body language accurately is a useful skill – and one that many interviewers have never been trained in or mastered! Unless students have done media studies they will not have formal training in this. The following exercise requires them to 'read' the visual signs and signifiers of a person and to categorize that person according to his or her profession. Encourage the students not to guess but to try to justify the reasons for their answers.

Aim To give the students the opportunity to practise the skills of reading both body language and other signifiers such as clothes and hairstyles.

Benefit To understand the power of body language and clothes as a determinant of people's opinions.

Materials required:
- Photocopies of handout 13:1 and Six Tips for each individual
- Flip chart, whiteboard or paper to record ideas and actions

Session plan
1 Introduce the concepts of body language, stereotyping and friend or foe (see 'What the experts say' on page 122).
2 Ask the students if they have ever been aware of sending out signals about themselves.
3 Ask them if this body-reading skill might be useful to busy people in a diverse society, or if it might be detrimental.
4 Give the students the handout and ask them to write down what profession they think each person belongs to and answer the questions about assumptions. Ask them to give reasons for their answers, referring to the signifiers in the pictures.
5 Ask the students to work in small groups and to compare their answers. Ask them to record the matching answers, if any, and to try to work out why they differed on the rest – for example, because of different life experiences or cultures.
6 Plenary:
   - What similarities did they find?
   - Does this tell us something about shared signs and common gender and race stereotypes?
   - Did they have any comments about the body language of the people in the pictures? Were there any shared understandings?
   - What does this tell us?
   - What does this tell us about going to an interview?
   - What should they take into account when planning what to wear at an interview?

Stereotyping

What assumptions do you make about these people from their appearance? Can you make any assumptions about the type of person they are? Do they conform to any stereotypes?

1

2

3

4

5

Exercise 13:2 Your 'elevator pitch'

In business, people practise a short speech for when people ask them questions in the elevator, or at a cocktail party, or interview. Questions such as 'Who are you?', 'What do you do?' or 'What do you want to do?'. This exercise is crucial to the development of confidence for facing interviews and introducing yourself to people. The 'elevator pitch' is a skill that not many adults master and one which will be valuable to young people for the rest of their lives. If you have time for only one exercise, this will be the most beneficial.

Aim To give students the opportunity to develop and to practise their own 'elevator pitches'.

Benefit Practising in advance means that they can introduce themselves with style (and without stuttering).

Materials required:
- Photocopies of handout 13:2 (see *www.networkpress.co.uk/resources* for colour version) and Six Tips for each individual.
- Pens and paper
- Whiteboard or paper for recording learning

Session plan
1 Introduce the concept of the 'elevator pitch'.
2 Ask the students to write a short speech that takes about 30 seconds and sounds natural, concentrating on the qualities that make them sound interesting. Remind them to highlight their unique selling points. What makes them tick?
3 Ask the students to practise it aloud. Try smiling!!
4 In pairs, get the students to introduce themselves to each other. If you have a brave, confident pair they could demonstrate to the rest of the class.
5 Plenary:
   - Think of as many places as possible where you will be able to use this technique.
   - How did it feel introducing yourself in this way?
   - Did the practice help?
   - How did it feel hearing your friend introduce himself or herself in this way?
   - How will this affect your preparation for interviews?

Your elevator speech

Write a short speech, to last about 30 seconds, introducing yourself.

- Imagine that you meet someone who asks you who you are, what you are currently doing at school and what you enjoy doing in your spare time.

- Include anything that is special about you.

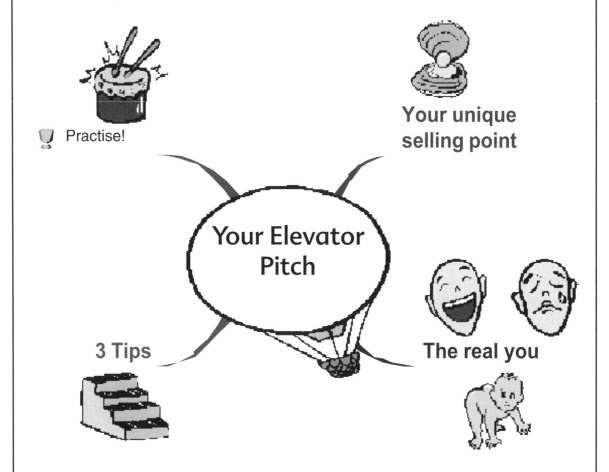

- Use the Mind Map® to help you to write about yourself.
- Try to add some comments on each branch about yourself.
- Practise saying this to a friend.

Three tips
- Remember your body language
- Look them in the eye
- Smile.

Exercise 13:3 Who would you give the job to?

Students are always keen to practise their skills in a safe environment and this exercise gives them the opportunity to be the interviewer and make a decision. They must assess three candidates for a job and select one of them, giving the reasons for their choice.

Aim To give the students the opportunity to experience how interviewers make decisions.

Benefit To understand that it is not always academic qualifications that lead to a person being successful – presentation makes a difference.

Materials required:
• Photocopies of handout 13:3 and Six Tips for each group of students
• Flip chart, whiteboard or paper to record ideas

Session plan
1 Introduce the concept of role-playing and interview panels.
2 Ask the students to get into groups of four or five and tell them that they will be an interview panel.
3 Give them the handout and ask them to decide which of the three candidates described should get the job.
4 Explain that their decisions must be unanimous and that they must give valid reasons for their decisions.
5 Take feedback from each group and record their comments on the board or on paper.
6 Plenary:
   ■ How did it feel reaching their decisions?
   ■ Was it easy or difficult to give reasons?
   ■ Were there any common reasons why the person was awarded the job? If so, what?
   ■ What does this tell us about how interviewers reach decisions?

The interview – who would you give the job to?

Work through the steps listed below. This is how Human Resources consider candidates. Draw up a chart of:

1 The skills required for the job.

2 How the candidates' qualifications and experience meet these requirements.

3 Also consider what personality the ideal candidate would have.

4 Finally, make a decision of who you would give the job to and why.

The company: a manufacturer making car seat covers

The job: general administration assistant

Duties:
- Photocopying
- Liaising with the public, answering phone
- Dealing with the post
- Organizing the annual holiday rota
- Helping to plan the Annual Golf Day

The three candidates
Assuming that the three candidates all perform the same at the interview, after it is over you are left with the following facts about them:

Candidate 1
Girl 19
Qualifications: 2 A levels, English and History
Experience: Saturday job 6 months in newsagents
Hobbies: netball, tennis, travel — spent 3 months travelling in Europe on Euro Rail

Candidate 2
Boy 17
Qualifications: 4 GCSEs A – C
Experience: 1 year postboy in mail room of insurance company; paper round for 2 months
Hobbies: driving, golf

Candidate 3
Girl 24
Qualifications: 3 GCSEs; Nursery Nurse Certificate
Experience: 2½ years admin assistant in builders' company
Hobbies: dancing and parties

Future Directions © Diane Carrington and Helen Whitten (Network Educational Press, 2005)

Preparing for interviews and meetings

Six Tips

1   Do careful research into what the interviewer might be looking for.

2   Make sure you know where the interview is and how long it will take to get there.

3   Plan some questions that you can ask the interviewer about the organization or the job.

4   Work out what you are going to wear; choose something appropriate for the job and the organization and that you feel comfortable in.

5   Remember, an interviewer is trying to see if you would fit in with the organization.

6   Try to enjoy the interview, this person wants to talk about you. Even if you don't enjoy it, try to smile!

Why bother?

- Whenever you meet people you make an impression. It is up to you what that impression is going to be. The more you practise at introducing yourself the better you will become. Remember, your body language, tone of voice and what you wear will always give a message about you, and you need to make sure that that message is a positive one.

- You need to have a plan to prepare not just what you are going to do and say but how you are going to look and how you are going to do and say it. Therefore it is essential to plan, prepare and rehearse.

- It is also important to see each interview as a learning opportunity to hone your interview skills and your ability to articulate your strengths and skills in a way that is true to you.

My first action step

Commit yourself to one action step over the next week that will help you to prepare for an interview.

This week I shall:

....

....

....

....

....

....

Section 3
Starting work

14 Setting expectations of work

We love to expect, and when expectation is either disappointed or gratified,
we want to be expecting again.

SAMUEL JOHNSON (1709–1784)

MOST YOUNG PEOPLE say that they simply did not know what to expect in their first weeks at work. It can be a challenging time and finding the right balance between not expecting too much and yet not expecting too little can be difficult. This chapter aims to help students identify some of the aspects of a company or work culture that will give them clues as to what to expect. They will also be given help in how to research this information.

The benefits of setting expectations of work

Learning to identify goals and expectations that are rational but neither too high nor too low can help students to find their way in a variety of situations. They will also come to realize that everyone sees the world differently. What they see as a reasonable expectation of how they should behave at work may not be seen in the same way by another person. Learning to value and respect these different perspectives not only helps young people manage themselves in their first weeks at work but can also help them to build relationships that are respectful of other people's differences.

As discussed in Chapter 5, expectations can influence how someone feels about a situation. Setting balanced expectations can prepare students for many aspects of work, such as:

■ fitting into the working culture;
■ knowing what to wear;
■ knowing whether the workplace culture values the status quo or innovation;
■ understanding what type of behaviours are expected of them and valued;
■ knowing how to succeed within the specific work they have chosen.

What the experts say

Psychologists have written about the power of expectations and the impact they can have on behaviour. As illustrated in Chapter 5, cognitive behavioural psychology identifies expectations of self, others and situations as being a major source of stress.

Expecting too much of yourself can lead to disappointment; expecting too little can lead to underachievement and lack of ambition. Achieving this balance is also important when having expectations of other people. If you have too high expectations it can lead to disappointment and conflict; and if you have too low expectations of people they may behave like doormats. The same applies to situations in general. For example, too low expectations can lead to underestimating the importance of, say, a tutorial or, in the workplace, a regular team meeting. Of course, low expectations can lead also to pleasant surprises and high expectations can lead to positive results, but a balanced, rational and optimistic outlook has been proven to more frequently produce both happiness and results.

Professor Martin Seligman (1990) has written extensively on the power of optimism to bring results in both work and relationships. Expectations that are positive and yet not pitched too high can mean that if you perceive someone can achieve something, then they can. Similarly, if you set yourself a high, but realistic, goal and believe you can do it you are more likely to be successful.

Neuro-Linguistic Programming has demonstrated how one person sees the world differently from another and, therefore, that what one person expects of a situation is often very different from what someone else might expect. One can never assume that someone else will share your viewpoint and one must seek to find out how another sees the situation in order to gauge their expectations of you.

A story to share

Suzie was a graduate who had done very well at both school and university. She had very high expectations of how she should be treated in her first job and believed she should be given responsible and high-profile work in her first few weeks. Instead, she was asked to courier papers and reports from one department to another, to do some photocopying and bring in the sandwiches for a client meeting.

She felt that these tasks were beneath her and she challenged her boss, Mary, saying that she was not being treated with the respect she deserved. Mary took her into her office and explained to Suzie that although she was a high-achiever in academic life she needed to realize that the demands that would be made of her in the workplace were different. She told Suzie she did not yet understand enough about the business and its requirements to be able to be given responsibility for projects. This meant that she would need to accept that she had much still to learn about the business and her role within it – this was not disrespectful, simply a fact of life. Mary said that she was aware of Suzie's potential and would help her to develop this only when she had demonstrated that she could manage the simple tasks first.

This was a hard lesson for Suzie, but she then understood that it was difficult for her boss to delegate tasks before she felt Suzie was ready for them.

Three steps to setting expectations of work

The three exercises here are designed to help young people to know how to identify the likely behaviours that will be expected of them as and when they start work.

Exercise 14:1 Work expectations

Before students go for interviews or start work it is helpful for them to have identified some of the factors of work culture so that they can (a) choose work that aligns with their personality and goals; and (b) seek to meet some of the expectations of that workplace.

Aim To start students thinking about what a workplace might expect of its employees.

Benefit When students know what to expect within a work setting they can feel more confident that they are doing the 'right' thing to make a good first impression.

Materials required:
- Photocopies of handouts 14:1:1 and 14:1:2 and Six Tips for each individual
- Advertisements from newspapers and magazines; cuttings about public and private sector workplaces; job advertisements; website links for the students to check before class
- Flip chart and/or board or paper for collage of information

Session plan
1 Explain that in Chapter 5 we discussed the fact that expectations shape emotions and experiences and that different views of a situation can lead to misunderstanding.

2 Introduce the fact that each workplace will have a set of expectations of its employees and that this can frequently be identified through specific clues in the language of advertisements and 'corporate' literature about the business and its products or services.

3 Put people into groups of four and give each group some literature, advertisements, press cuttings, annual reports or information from two different organizations.

4 The groups should consider and identify the following:
- What type of culture might this organization have?
- What might the organization expect of its employees in terms of dress/behaviours?
- Would the working environment be formal/informal?
- Is the organization service-oriented/profit-oriented?
- Is its focus on innovation/status quo?
- Is the work individualistic/team-based?
- Will the students' knowledge and ideas be valued?
- Is it a 'hierarchical' organization?
- What might be organizational 'taboos' (what is unacceptable to talk about)?
- What might be discussed at coffee machines/shared desks?

5 Explain that they will not be able to 'know' these answers but that they can intuitively pick up some of this information from the literature you have provided.

6 Give the groups 15 minutes to prepare a two-minute presentation explaining the likely culture and expectations that they have deduced about each company.

7 Plenary:
- Do they think it is possible to gauge the expectations a company might have of them from literature of this sort?
- How might this information be applied? For example, would it help them to decide what to wear, or what to do and say at an interview/first week at work?
- Suggest that if they are considering a specific career, they could research information about that organization on the internet and bring any comments or questions to future sessions.

Work expectations

Entering an organization where people have been working for some time in a particular way can be challenging. Before accepting a job, and before starting your first day at work, it is helpful to take some time to consider the culture of the organization.

Workplace culture is 'the way people do things' in that environment. It is the feeling you get from visiting a workplace and from brand advertising. For example, a company like BT has quite a different feel from Orange; British Airways a different culture from Virgin or Easyjet. Even visiting various supermarkets will give you a feel of corporate cultures and how they can differ. One school is different from another; one hospital has its own unique 'feel'. Local government in Manchester will feel and do things differently from local government in rural Devon.

When you go to an interview, decide on a career or start your first day at work it is helpful to know if an organization has a culture you like and respect. Similarly, it is helpful to work out how you could 'fit in'. Respecting the way things are currently done can help you to integrate at the beginning.

Below is a checklist to complete when considering your future workplace. Try to answer these questions in as much detail as possible and give evidence for your answers from the advertisements:

- What type of culture might this organization have?
- What is a word to describe the culture of the organization? (Is it formal/informal?)
- What do the logo, brand and 'strapline' say about the organization?
- Is it service-oriented/profit-oriented?
- Does it focus on innovation/status quo?
- Is it a 'hierarchical' organization?
- How should you address the hierarchy?
- Will your creative ideas be valued?
- Is knowledge highly valued?
- Is profit highly valued?
- Is the work individualistic/team-based?
- Will order, discipline and structure be important?
- Who are the customers?
- What might the organization expect of its employees in terms of:

    a) dress code;

    b) behaviours;

    c) 'taboos' (for example, what is unacceptable to talk about)?

- What might be frequently heard statements or conversation at coffee machines/shared desks?

Future Directions © Diane Carrington and Helen Whitten (Network Educational Press, 2005)

Hints about dress codes

- Unless you are someone who is deciding to go into the workplace and be noticed as different, then it can help to check out the customs regarding what to wear.

- Even 'establishment' organizations such as banking, the law and accountancy have relaxed these days and a tie/suit are not always necessary. Many companies have 'dress down' policies, so you may need to have some 'smart casual' outfits to wear — not jeans and T-shirts but smarter trousers/skirt with a shirt or jumper, for example.

- If you are going into manual work or a more hands-on service-oriented workplace then check out how informal you can be.

- One thing that many of the more traditional organizations seem to agree on is that tights/stockings are more professional than bare legs but, again, each workplace is different — so check them out.

- If you want to be taken seriously, consider the impact your clothes may have on other people. As we have explained elsewhere, you have only one chance to make a good first impression and it is helpful to remember that you are being noticed every day, every time you walk along a corridor or get a cup of coffee.

- Ask your future boss, or the HR manager or a prospective colleague what is expected so that you can make a decision you feel comfortable with. It is certainly important to choose clothes that make you feel happy, confident and at your best.

- Finally, think of practical questions to ask before you start. For example, if you are going to a construction company, will you need a hard hat? If you are going into a medical or scientific organization will you need overalls?

Exercise 14:2 Relationship expectations

Building relationships in life and in the workplace is crucial to success. Understanding the pressures, concerns and expectations of others will help a young person to fit in and develop harmonious relationships from the outset.

Aim To help students understand how different people have different expectations of other people's behaviour and of specific situations.

Benefit Understanding and valuing difference is an important relationship skill in school and in work. We live in an interdependent world where valuing other people's contributions is essential for the performance of any team and organization.

Materials required:
- Photocopies of handout 14:2 and Six Tips for each individual
- Flip chart or paper to collect feedback

Session plan

1 Explain that we all develop expectations of ourselves, other people and behaviour in general from the moment we are born. In the main, we develop these from our parents, family and early authority figures. Inevitably, culture, nationality and environment also continue to shape our expectations and perspectives of behaviour but the net result is that we all see the world differently. As they grow up, the students can define what their own expectations of others are, as opposed to those that other people hold.

2 People can pick up clues about expectations from the language someone uses, particularly from words such as 'must', 'should', 'ought to'. For example, if Mary says 'John SHOULD say thank you for the present I sent him' this means that Mary's expectations are, in general, that 'people should thank for birthday presents'. Jeremy might comment, 'I must wear a suit for my interview', which denotes that Jeremy's expectation is that suits are appropriate wear for interviews. Suggest the group share some more ideas on this theme.

3 Explain that when the students enter the workplace, their bosses and colleagues will have certain expectations of their behaviour and that it will be helpful for them to learn to (a) understand other people's perspectives; (b) value and respect them; and (c) learn to build relationships with people who may have very different perspectives and expectations from their own.

4 Give the students the handout. Allow them ten minutes on their own to consider the situation and try to identify what each person might have been expecting of the other.

5 Put students into pairs and get them to discuss the situation further.

6 Plenary:
   - Ask students to share their thoughts on what the characters in the case situation were expecting of each other.
   - Ask them to identify how the people might build harmonious relationships, despite differences of opinion and viewpoint.
   - Ask them to identify how they personally might seek to understand and value the opinions of others in future.

Relationship expectations

People build up expectations of life and other people that may be quite different from your own. In order to identify what other people's expectations are start to notice words such as: **'should'**, **'must'** or **'ought to'**.

These often betray people's expectations of the behaviour of others. We tend to see the world from our own ideal perspective — how we would like life to be; how we would prefer others to behave.

In the workplace, you will meet a variety of people from diverse cultures. You will need to build relationships with people who have different viewpoints from your own. Their perspective may be different, but valid.

Read the story below and consider what expectation each person has of the situation. Try to imagine how they feel and also how you would feel if you were involved. Answer the questions that follow the story.

Case situation

Simon's boss, Matt, has taken him and another new recruit, Angie, out to lunch in their first week at work. Matt has taken them to a pub and Simon orders a pint of beer and then notices that neither Matt nor Angie have ordered alcohol. Simon feels uncomfortable but it seems natural for him to drink alcohol if they are in a pub. He decides to drink it slowly and they start to talk. About five minutes into the conversation, Matt brings a tray of sandwiches for them all. Matt has not asked what people want to eat and Angie finds that there are no vegetarian sandwiches. Unsure what to do, she takes a sandwich and eats just the crust. Matt's mobile phone goes off and he answers it and then turns it off. Shortly afterwards, Simon's mobile phone also goes off and Simon answers it and talks for a while before hanging up. As the trio continue their conversation, Simon's mobile rings again and he talks to this caller as well. While Matt is paying the bill Simon receives two text messages and looks at them. Simon does not offer to share the bill. Matt is getting visibly annoyed but does not say anything. They leave the pub and walk back to work.

List the areas of confusion among these three people and give their different perspectives:

What hindered the communication? ....

....

....

What would have helped? ....

....

....

Future Directions © Diane Carrington and Helen Whitten (Network Educational Press, 2005)

Exercise 14:3 High–low expectations

Many students have watched Hollywood movies and soaps where doctors, teachers and business executives are portrayed as celebrity characters who are rich and successful. This can lead young people to imagine that getting a job means immediate power and status whereas, of course, the reality is that most people start at the beginning and make their way up.

Aim To give students the opportunity to consider how to develop balanced and reasonable expectations of how they might be treated as they enter the workplace.

Benefit It is helpful to develop rational and positive expectations. As we have discussed before, having over-high expectations can be unrealistic and lead to disappointment; to have too low expectations can limit the development of talent and potential.

Materials required:
- Photocopies of handout 14:3 and Six Tips for each individual
- Flip chart or paper to collect ideas

Session plan
1 Explain how expectations can become unrealistic if one imagines that one is going to get a high-status and responsible job the minute one arrives.
2 However, students need to value and identify their own qualifications, contribution and status so as not to be treated like doormats.
3 If one has a disability or belongs to a minority culture, it is possible to expect that one's options are limited. In fact, there are plenty of inspiring stories of people who have overcome their limited expectations to achieve great things for themselves.
4 Put the students in twos and give them the handouts. Allow them ten minutes to respond to the questions and another five minutes to discuss their thoughts and findings.
5 Plenary:
   - How can the students make sure that they achieve their personal potential without expecting too much too soon?
   - What would be courteous ways of explaining to a boss that one can do more useful tasks than making the coffee?
   - How can you encourage each other to raise personal expectations so as to achieve goals?

High–low expectations

There is a balance to be struck between expectations of yourself that are too low — doing all the menial chores all the time — and those that are too high — expecting to be the managing director before you have even been there a short time.

You may have done very well academically, but work involves a different set of skills and concepts. You need to recognize that it is necessary for you to be an 'apprentice' for some time, while you get to understand the requirements expected of you. Even managing directors have to make the coffee and do the photocopying from time to time, so try to accept those activities and observe how they may help you to learn more about the business or organization. However, equally, you don't want to accept too little for yourself and if you find yourself being given too many low-grade activities it is possible to explain that you have ways to contribute more.

Questionnaire

1   Have you ever had any expectations of yourself at school?

   ....

   If so list three expectations:

   ....

   Have you ever failed to achieve your expectations? Yes/No

   How did this make you feel? ....

   Looking back on it, was it a realistic goal? ....

   How did you manage this experience? ....

   What did you learn that might be useful for the future? ....

   ....

2   Have you ever achieved more than your expectations?...

   How did this make you feel? ....

   Looking back on it, was it a realistic goal? ....

   How did you manage this experience? ....

   What did you learn that might be useful for the future?

   ....

3   How can you get the balance of high–low expectations right? Which of the following coping mechanisms would help?

   • setting realistic goals;

   • knowing your strengths and weaknesses;

   • being flexible;

   • learning from mistakes;

   • having positive and optimistic expectations but not being fixed on the result;

   • not being over-influenced by other people;

   • being true to yourself.

Think whether you could apply any of these coping mechanisms to situations you have experienced in the past. You could use your examples from Questions 1 and 2 above.

Future Directions © Diane Carrington and Helen Whitten (Network Educational Press, 2005)

Setting expectations of work

Six Tips

1 Learn to identify and understand the work culture of the prospective companies you are targeting, as this will help you know how to behave, communicate and dress appropriately.

2 Recognize that people behave in many different ways, each one justified. There is no 'right' way. Observe and identify differences and respect other people's way of doing things, just as they can respect yours.

3 Balance your expectations so that they are not so high as to always disappoint and not so low that you never take a risk or accept a challenge. Expectations shape your emotions, so become more aware of your thinking.

4 Listen to the words 'must', 'should', 'ought to' as these denote the expectations that people have of themselves, other people and situations in general.

5 Remember that other people are busy and are not necessarily being unfriendly if they don't give you time. Be sensitive to their needs but at the same time don't neglect your own.

6 Don't take things too personally!

Why bother?

■ Much conflict arises as a result of mismatched expectations. For example, if an employee thinks that the most important duty is to complete the meeting minutes but the boss thinks the most important duty is to carry out customer research then the employee could be putting energy into the wrong task.

■ Taking the initiative to clarify expectations of your role and performance can pay dividends in making sure you are putting your energy into the priority tasks. It is important not to assume that you know what another person expects of you.

■ In a relationship, if a husband expects that his wife will cook his supper but she feels her most important duty is to earn a salary and contribute to the home, he will be disappointed.

■ It is therefore important that you also share your expectations of other people and situations with those around you as otherwise this can lead to confusion.

My first action step

Commit yourself to one action step over the next week that will help you to set rational expectations of work.

This week I shall:

....

....

....

....

....

15 Managing day-to-day living

We are what we repeatedly do. Excellence, then, is not an act but a habit.

ARISTOTLE (384–322BC)

YOUNG PEOPLE often become used to their parents or teachers taking responsibility for organizing their lives. As they grow up and leave home they have to learn to take responsibility for themselves. This includes their health, their time-keeping, their relationships, their performance at work, and the organization of many practical things on a daily basis. This chapter is designed to help the students identify practical areas that they will need to manage as they make the transition into the adult world.

The benefits of managing day-to-day living

The more young people can learn to have their affairs in order at an early age, the more prepared they are likely to feel as they begin work. Being unsure where important papers are filed, or how to lay hands on a phone bill or credit card bill, can result in confusion and fuzzy thinking.

Humans readily form habits of behaviour and it is harder to alter entrenched habits at a later stage of life than it is to start off in a disciplined way. Learning early on to deal with filing, time management, paying bills promptly and being generally organized saves time and stress at a later date. It can also save money, as late payment of bills can result in high interest rates and debt.

What the experts say

Government and other organizations, such as the NHS, banks, telecommunications companies and debt agencies, advise people to ensure that they have their affairs up to date and in order. The consequences of not doing so can be expensive. For example, if someone has not kept up credit card payments he or she can be charged hefty sums in interest. If you don't get your tax form in on time you can be fined and even have a criminal record. If you become ill but are not registered with a doctor, you may be jeopardizing your health.

Getting things in order is important and allows people to feel secure. They can then concentrate on other aspects of their lives because they have minimized the risk of things going wrong. Dave Allen, Stephen Covey and Alvin Hall have all written on these subjects (websites for Allen and Covey are included in *Resources* on page 191).

A story to share

Joseph threw all his mail and bills into a drawer in his bedroom, sometimes without even looking at them. He always felt there were better things to do with his life and was busy enjoying himself and also working for his degree. His father put money into his bank account and Joseph assumed that this would cover his credit card and mobile phone payments. He never bothered to check until he woke up one night and realized that the envelope he had received that morning had a 'bailiff's notice' on it. He opened it up and saw that his car was about to be repossessed because his standing order had not been paid for four months.

  By the time he got down to the street the next morning to check it out the car had already been towed away by the bailiffs. Joseph then had to go through all the papers in the drawer to find out what had gone wrong. It turned out that he had overspent on his credit card and that his bank account was overdrawn, so the standing orders had not been paid. It was an expensive lesson, and after sorting out the problem he vowed never to allow the situation to get as bad again in future.

Three steps to managing day-to-day living

The three exercises in this chapter give students some time to consider different areas of their lives in order to become more organized and efficient in managing practicalities.

Exercise 15:1 Practicalities checklist

This is a checklist to help students identify which areas of their lives are in order and which areas they still have to organize. They also need to realize that these items will change should they move house, get married, or their financial circumstances alter.

Aim To help students identify areas of their lives that need organizing, such as registering with a doctor, ensuring that they complete a self-assessment tax form and so on. This is not a definitive list but will help them to start to think about what they need to manage.

Benefit To have a one-page summary of information, where they can see at a glance areas of their lives that they have and have not organized. In this way they can decide to take action and stay in control.

Materials required:
• Photocopies of handout 15:1 and Six Tips for each individual
• Flip chart, whiteboard or paper to record ideas and actions

Session plan
1 Introduce the fact that as they grow up and leave home they have to take personal responsibility for keeping their affairs in order.
2 Ask them to brainstorm the type of practicalities they will need to consider and manage.
3 Capture these ideas on a flip chart, whiteboard or on paper.
4 Give the students the checklist and allow them five minutes to study the list. They should tick areas they have completed and put in dates with regard to actions they still need to take. They will not necessarily have the contact details or account numbers with them – explain that they can complete the list later at home.
5 Once they have completed the list individually, put them in threes and ask them to consider the implications of not having these things in order.
6 Plenary:
   ■ How does it feel to plan these things?
   ■ How confident do they feel that they already have their affairs in reasonable order?
   ■ What ideas can they share about how to maintain this list in good order?

Practicalities checklist

Go down the list and tick off areas you have already organized. Where you still have to arrange the item, put in a date as a goal.

ITEM	DONE/ NOT DONE	DATE TO ARRANGE BY	RENEWAL DATE	CONTACT DETAILS AND ACCOUNT NUMBERS
Registered with doctor				
Identified nearest A & E Dept				
Registered for self-assessment tax				
Registered with dentist				
National Insurance no.				
Personal insurance				
Travel insurance				
Home and contents insurance				
Car tax				
Car insurance				
TV licence				
Telephone contract				
Mobile contract				
Gas				
Electricity				
Bank account				
Internet/broadband				
Council tax				
Employment contract				
Gym membership				
Pension				

Note down those actions you still need to take and put a note in your diary on specific dates when you have the time to arrange them.

Future Directions © Diane Carrington and Helen Whitten (Network Educational Press, 2005)

Exercise 15:2 Getting organized at home and work

This exercise helps young people to decide how to manage practicalities at home and at work. This includes paperwork, housework, shopping, cooking and preparing for work.

Aim To encourage students to take control of their environment at home and at work and to see that this will help them to live their lives harmoniously. To help them plan where they need to take action.

Benefit To see that a home can provide sustenance and refreshment after a busy working day and that returning to chaos is not much fun.

Materials required:
- Photocopies of handout 15:2 and Six Tips for each individual
- Flip chart, whiteboard or paper to record ideas
- Video/DVD (for example, of *The Young Ones* or *Withnail and I*, which illustrate young people living in chaos!)

Session plan
1 Introduce the fact that they will now have to become organized in housekeeping as well as keeping their filing and their desks at work tidy.
2 If you have a DVD then show them a clip or two and discuss the state in which the characters kept their flat. If you haven't got the clip, discuss generally how it is often considered trendy for college students and young people to live in chaos and 'boring' to be organized.
3 Give them the handout and allow them five or ten minutes to answer the questions.
4 Put them in twos and ask them to discuss how prepared they feel for managing these everyday factors of life.
5 Plenary:
   - What did students' answers say about them?
   - Do these areas matter, or are they happy to be disorganized? How might this affect their lives?
   - What percentage of the group feel confident that they will manage well?
   - What could they do to help themselves become more organized and confident? For example, perhaps they could start to take control of these factors immediately – even if they are living at home they could, say, cook for the family once a week.
   - Could they teach themselves to manage more effectively?
   - Is there someone who could give them some training or support?

Getting organized at home and work

You may be thinking about leaving home and setting up on your own or sharing a flat or house with friends. Maintaining a balanced and orderly home life gives you a sanctuary to return to in the evenings after a long day's work. Piles of dirty washing-up are no fun at 7am in the morning, as you get yourself ready for work. Ten minutes a day can help you have a home to be proud of.

Answer the following questions:

Home activity	Yes	No
Do you prefer to keep your room tidy?	☐	☐
Do you do the washing-up as soon as you have eaten?	☐	☐
Do you own and use a vacuum cleaner?	☐	☐
Do you do your own washing and ironing?	☐	☐
Would you describe yourself as an organized person?	☐	☐

You are what you eat
What and how you eat directly affect your physical and mental well-being, so choose the fresh and healthy options (companies will pay less money if you are ill for a long period of time).

Answer the following questions:

Food choices and cooking	Yes	No
Do you know how to boil an egg?	☐	☐
Do you eat fresh fruit and vegetables?	☐	☐
Can you cook a meal for friends?	☐	☐
Do you drink plenty of water and fresh juices?	☐	☐
Do you feel confident in your cooking ability?	☐	☐

Time and paperwork
Becoming efficient in how you manage your time and organize your paperwork is essential to your future success. Answer the following questions:

Time organization	Yes	No
Are you generally on time for appointments?	☐	☐
Do you allow any extra time for the unexpected when planning a route to work or a meeting?	☐	☐
Do you have an efficient filing system?	☐	☐
Do you know where your bank statements are filed?	☐	☐
Do you feel confident in your organizational skills?	☐	☐

If you have answered 9 or more 'Yes' then you are well prepared for the future. If you have answered 9 or more 'No' then you need to take action to become organized.

Exercise 15:3 I want to be a millionaire

This exercise assumes individuals have some control over money. It flags up the fact that taking time out to identify the best way to manage money pays off in the long run. It helps young people consider how to budget, how to stay out of debt and how to make their money grow.

Aim To help students realize that money management does not happen by itself and that they need to take action if they are to ensure that their money is safe and grows.

Benefit Achieving financial security.

Materials required:
- Photocopies of handout 15:3 and Six Tips for each individual
- Flip chart, whiteboard or paper to record ideas and actions

Session plan
1   Explain that money management is an important factor in happiness, security and success.
2   Brainstorm some of the factors that students will need to consider in terms of managing their money – for example, salary level, weekly savings, budgeting, outgoings such as rent and transport, tax, National Insurance.
3   Give them the handout. Ask them to look at the budget sheet and consider their own lives and how they might start to manage their money.
4   Put them in twos and tell them to look at the questions on the handout. Explain that one of them will role-play a Financial Adviser who will ask some pertinent questions. The other person will role-play the Client. At the end of the questions they will have some time to brainstorm ideas about how to become a millionaire and make good use of their money. They can have ten minutes each way.
5   Plenary:
    - Do they feel that they are already well on the way to managing their money?
    - What ideas did they have as a group for saving and increasing their money?
    - Have any of them checked out interest rates and ensured that their money is in the right place?
    - Do they budget?
    - How can they ensure they do not get into debt?

I want to be a millionaire

Whether or not you really do want to be a millionaire you will need to think carefully about your money in order to achieve financial security and be able to live the life you want.

In twos, take the following exercise in turns. One person is the Client and the other the Financial Adviser. The Financial Adviser asks the Client the following questions (take ten minutes each way):

- Do you have your money in a bank account?
- Do you put savings into a deposit account or building society?
- Have you checked that you are getting the best interest you can on this money?
- Do you budget regularly?
- Have you started to put money aside for a mortgage?
- Have you started to put money aside for a pension?
- Have you planned how you will pay off your student loan?
- Do you plan for a rainy day?
- Do you save for holidays and unexpected events?
- How will you budget to ensure that you don't overspend?
- How can you plan for the long-term future, such as buying your first home?
- Do you pay off your credit card on time every month?
- How do you record the dates on which payments need to be made?
- Have you got any debts or loans?
- How will you plan to pay these off step by step?

Now, together, brainstorm ideas to help the Client to manage his or her money efficiently — for example, going on the internet to check out the best banking service and interest rates.

Now swop places.
Record action points below:

1 ....
2 ....
3 ....

Budgeting spreadsheet

Income		Clothes	....
Salary	....	Travel	....
Allowance	....	Holidays	....
Other	....	CDs	....
Total:	....	Telephone	....
		Gas	....
Outgoings		Electricity	....
Rent	....	Water	....
Food	....	Council tax	....
Cosmetics	....	Insurance	....
Stationery	....	Other	....
Books	....	Total:	....
Drink	....		
Leisure	....	Total left per month:	
Gym	....	Spending per week:	

Managing day-to-day living

Six Tips

1 Practise getting to work on time by leaving home early enough. Work out the best transport system to use.

2 Start keeping home and paperwork tidy and filing in order, now.

3 Save, budget and plan to be a millionaire!

4 Plan how you will pay off any loans or student loans.

5 Make a diary note for when credit card payments are due to ensure that you do not accrue interest.

6 Look for what you can save each week – small things (a cola, cigarettes) cost money. Just one cappuccino can cost as much as £2.50 – multiply that by seven and it comes to £17.50. Do you really want to spend that much on coffee each week?

Why bother?

- Getting into debt is a miserable experience. Planning carefully how you spend your money each week will help you to do the things you want to do. Money is not the be-all and end-all of life, but it certainly helps.

- Attention to detail can make the difference in terms of making your money grow and ensuring that you do not fritter it away on unnecessary or small things.

- The housing market is worth entering at some stage. Start saving for your deposit as soon as you are able.

My first action step

Commit yourself to one action step over the next week that will help you to manage day-to-day living.

This week I shall:

....

....

....

....

....

....

....

....

16 Contributing at work

New occasions teach new duties...
JAMES RUSSELL LOWELL (1819–1891)

Young people can often be unsure about how much they will be able to contribute when they first start work. They imagine that everyone else is very proficient and knows what he or she is doing, and so they fear that they might be the only ones who don't know what to do. Of course, this isn't the case and it can be helpful for them to realize that becoming a success in the role they have chosen in life is an evolving process and does not happen on Day One.

It may interest them to know that many senior people – even chief executives of major worldwide companies – frequently feel inadequate and are uncomfortable with the fact that many younger people have more qualifications than they do. In fact, in today's world of global competition, the larger organizations tend to look to smaller entrepreneurial businesses for ideas – and that often means to younger people.

This chapter aims to help students identify what they might contribute in their first few weeks at work, and how to do so.

The benefits of knowing how to contribute at work

Students cannot articulate what they have to offer unless they identify what those things might be or recognize the situations in which they can contribute knowledge, ideas and energy. Situations where they can contribute from Day One of their working lives are:

- in relationships with others;
- in the energy and emotional enthusiasm they bring to a department or team;
- in meetings – with comments, challenges and ideas politely put;
- systems and technology;
- using initiative.

What the experts say

Creative productivity is the result of diversity of thought and approach. Ned Herrmann studied high-performing teams and observed that many were made up of different types of people. Edward de Bono has also made similar points in his many books on lateral thinking. A group made up of young and old, male and female, different thinkers and of a cultural diversity is inevitably going to have more ways of looking at situations than a group of people who are similar.

Young people have fluid intelligence and learn things quickly. They do not necessarily have the perspective of an older person and so are likely to draw different conclusions. This can challenge norms and add a vital ingredient to the creative mix of a team.

Stories to share

Many companies today are run by very young people who have come up with an entrepreneurial idea. In an era of technology, dotcom companies and rapidly changing design and fashion, young people can sometimes excel at gauging what other young people might want to do or buy.

The Innocent Smoothie company was started by two young men who had been working in the City but got bored with their jobs. They realized that every evening they were enjoying making themselves fruit juice drinks and decided to give up their day jobs and set up the Innocent Drinks Company. They have become a very successful business.

Richard Branson was 20 years old when he founded Virgin as a mail order record retailer and a short while later he opened a record shop in Oxford Street, London. In 1972, a recording studio was built in Oxfordshire where the first Virgin artist, Mike Oldfield, recorded 'Tubular Bells', later released in 1973. The first album of Virgin Records went on to sell more than five million copies. At the age of 27, Richard signed the Sex Pistols to the Virgin Records label after the group was turned down by every label in Great Britain.

Ben and Jerry's ice creams were the original idea of two school friends, Ben Cohen and Jerry Greenfield. Ben enrolled at university and dropped out; Jerry graduated, applied to medical school but ended up as a lab technician. The two friends decided to pursue their dream of starting a firm together, researched the industry, did a $5 course on ice cream making and set up their ice cream parlour.

Three steps to contributing at work

The following exercises can help young people to consider what they have to contribute in the workplace. These three steps also demonstrate how to identify the most appropriate situations, where individuals may be offered the opportunity to show what they can do.

Exercise 16:1 What do I have to contribute?

This short exercise, which builds on Section 1 of the book, is a good icebreaking introduction to the concept of unique contribution and can be used together with Exercises 14.2 and 14.3. It is important for young people to recognize that although they may not have experienced a great deal in their lives, the experiences they have had will have given them strengths. They will also have studied specific subjects at school, college, university or in an apprenticeship that will enable them to offer specialist knowledge.

Aim To help students identify their unique contribution to an organization.

Benefit To realize that others do not think like they do.

Materials required:
- Photocopies of handout 16:1 (see *www.networkpress.co.uk/resources* for colour version) and Six Tips for each individual
- Flip chart, whiteboard or paper to record ideas and actions

Session plan

1 Talk about the concept of contribution and help the students to brainstorm how they are contributing in class, at home, in a sports team, music group or with friends. Capture the ideas on a flip chart.

2 Now explain that they will need to build on these ideas and realize that they are unique in how their brains work. Give each student the handout. Explain that it will be a simple word association exercise and that – like the example they see on the page – they will be given a word and asked to freely associate from it.

3 Give them any word (tree, elephant, book, spring, holiday) and ask them to put that word on the first line and to freely associate the next words that come into their head from there. They do not have to stick logically to the theme of the first word (although some individuals may do so).

4 When they have completed this exercise, give them five minutes to take their pieces of paper and walk around the room or collaborate at their tables to compare their words with those of the other students. They will discover that everyone has a different series of words. This demonstrates their unique way of thinking and the need for them to value their ideas and input; they cannot make the assumption that 'someone else will have thought of this already', because no one else thinks like them.

5 Plenary:
- What have they noticed?
- Has anyone got the same last word?
- Have they got any words in common on their lists?
- Why do they think the answers are so varied?
- Can they value their unique viewpoint?
- What ideas do they have about how they might contribute at work?
- How does it feel to recognize that there has never been anyone who thinks exactly like you in the past; and there never will be anyone like you in the future?

Word association exercise

Look at the flow lines shown below. You will see that the top line demonstrates how one person's associations flowed from the word 'pen' along the line, each word giving rise to the next one. In a moment, your teacher will give you a word to put on the bottom line and ask you to write down your own random associations from that word.

When you have finished the line, and everyone else has finished, take this page and compare notes with other people. See whether you can find anyone with a brain exactly like yours.

Flow of Associations

Pen   paper   tv   Richard   safari   Sun

news   Friends   Lionheart

What did you notice about how your brain associates?

....

....

....

Now look at the following list. Tick words that relate to your way of thinking and might represent areas in which you could contribute at work:

Vision	Analysis	Mentoring
Energy	Problem solving	Technology
Enthusiasm	Ideas	Typing
Calm	Customer understanding	Spreadsheets
Organization	Language skills	IT
Specific knowledge	Science	Music
Patience	Design	Art
Tolerance	People	Social science
Listening skills	Practical skills	Media
Maths	Teaching	Communication

Future Directions © Diane Carrington and Helen Whitten (Network Educational Press, 2005)

Exercise 16:2 Where might you contribute?

This exercise allows students to identify a variety of situations and opportunities where they may be able to contribute. Unless they are prepared, they may miss opportunities to offer their initiative, as a moment passes by too quickly.

Aim To enable students to rehearse situations where they may be able to contribute their ideas, knowledge and skills at work.

Benefit Being mentally and emotionally prepared to meet a situation before it arises.

Materials required:
• Photocopies of handout 16:2 and Six Tips for each individual
• Flip chart, whiteboard or paper to record ideas and actions

Session plan
1 Give students the handout and ask them to brainstorm as many different situations as possible in which they could contribute. Allow them five minutes.
2 Put them in groups of six and give them another five minutes to think of more.
3 Plenary:
   ■ Share the ideas they have accumulated – ask each group to present their ideas in a list or Mind Map® format so that you can photocopy all the ideas at the end of the lesson.
   ■ How do they feel when they make a contribution?
   ■ Now that they have seen other people's lists, are there any other contributions they would like to make?
   ■ Can they give examples of how a school, sports team, band, village, workplace relies on contributions from many different people in order to function well?
   ■ Can they understand how unique everyone is by the fact that many people will have come up with similar ideas but each group has offered some new ideas (this is likely).
   ■ Do they now feel more prepared to contribute in different situations?

16:2

Contributions that I make

Complete the following sentences:

Contributions I make at home are:

....

....

Contributions I make at school are:

....

....

Contributions I make to my friends are:

....

....

Contributions I make to my family are:

....

....

Contributions I make in any other situation are:

....

....

....

....

....

....

Future Directions © Diane Carrington and Helen Whitten (Network Educational Press, 2005)

Exercise 16:3 If I were in charge I would...

This gives individuals the opportunity to consider what type of business they might like to start if given a chance; and where they might wish to contribute their ideas within education, the health service, social services, police and other organizations. They can create any scenario they please and put their ideas forward in a persuasive way in order to influence the situation.

Aim To give students the opportunity to practise expressing ideas in a persuasive manner.

Benefit Enables them to rehearse and act out the communication of their ideas and knowledge.

Materials required:
- Photocopies of handout 16:3 and Six Tips for each individual
- Large sheets of paper for each group
- Flip chart, whiteboard or paper

Session plan
1 Explain that they are going to have the opportunity to express their ideas about how a situation might be improved.
2 Give them the handout and put them in groups of four. Tell them that they can think of any organization or department that they might wish to be able to change or improve – for example, they could imagine that they are the new CEO of a large organization; or a new headteacher at a school; or a new head of the NHS, police force, social system, transport system, or the new prime minister.
3 In their groups they need to (a) decide the scenario; (b) consider what ideas they have for changing this organization or service for the better; (c) how they might go about expressing those ideas in a persuasive manner.
4 Explain that they will need to convey their credibility when they make their presentations.
5 Give them ten minutes to prepare their presentations, following the guidelines on the handout. Each member of the group needs to be involved.
6 Each group will then give a five-minute presentation.
7 Plenary:
   - How did it feel expressing ideas for improving a service or organization?
   - Were other people convinced?
   - How persuasive were they? (You could make it competitive.)
   - How might they have been more persuasive?

If I were in charge I would...

You are going to be given the opportunity to express your ideas for improvement of an organization, system, service, political group — or whatever you choose.

In your groups you need to:

(a) Identify an organization that you might want to improve. This could be a private or public sector organization; health service; bank; insurance; social services; police; NHS; airline; transport. YOU CAN CHOOSE.

(b) Brainstorm your ideas for how you might improve this service or organization IF YOU WERE IN CHARGE.

(c) Create a five-minute presentation that involves all four of you and is persuasive of your ideas.

(d) Give the presentation, conveying your credibility and the persuasiveness of your argument.

Feedback:
What did you learn? ....

....

....

What might you do better next time?...

....

....

....

How can you practise applying your ideas and opinions in future so that you contribute to improving life and work?

....

....

....

....

....

Contributing at work

Six Tips

1 You can contribute: ideas, physical help, emotions – such as enthusiasm – communication and support, knowledge and information, expertise.

2 Don't be backward in coming forward.

3 Remember that even if you are young and inexperienced you still have ideas to contribute at work.

4 Look for opportunities to improve the way people are working – perhaps by using practical or technical systems.

5 Agree guidelines with your boss about how you should spend downtime.

6 Speak up – share your thoughts, ideas, questions. All of these help other people to shape their own ideas and make decisions.

Why bother?

■ When you start work it can be difficult to know what people want you to do. Sometimes you may feel you are overqualified and other times you may feel you know nothing. So it helps to give shape to things you feel you can contribute and then you are ready and prepared when the moment arrives.

■ It is important to recognize that companies often need the fresh ideas of young people to drive the future. People get so used to working in a specific way that they can forget to question why they are doing it that way – it may well have started many years before, when life was very different. Take business as an example. In the Industrial Revolution, when most businesses were begun, it was an all-male environment and a local community. Now you have an international community of men and women with cultural differences and a huge variety of different ways of contributing ideas and action. Young people have grown up into this environment and have new perspectives to contribute.

My first action step

Commit yourself to one action step over the next week that will help you to learn how to contribute at work.

This week I shall:

....

....

....

....

....

....

....

Future Directions © Diane Carrington and Helen Whitten (Network Educational Press, 2005)

Section 4

Future direction

17 Achieving work–life balance

*No one ever said on his or her tombstone
'I wish I had spent more time at the office'.*

ANON

To work hard and play hard, makes Jack a bright lad.
TRADITIONAL NURSERY RHYME

YOUR STUDENTS will already appreciate that, today, life is full. They may have part-time jobs, as well as having coursework deadlines, sport and other extra-curricular activities, and see exams looming. They will also often see their parents' lives being frantic, working and managing homes, and see their teachers being placed under pressure. Therefore, it is helpful to encourage them to consider the work–life balance they would like to develop. The UK has the longest working hours in Europe and young people can feel pressurized to adopt the same work patterns as other people in the organization that they work in.

Work–life balance means different things to different people at different times in their lives. For a young person, it might be having the time to pursue a hobby or an interest, for an adult it might be having time to care for children or a sick relative. The important common element is that the individual's parallel needs are taken into consideration and acted upon where possible.

The benefits of achieving work–life balance

There are some important factors about work–life balance that may have a great impact on the lives of students. Some factors that might affect them are given below:

- Over-working can lead to ill-health through fatigue and exhaustion.
- Tiredness leads to mistakes.
- You may choose to focus on one priority, but it may not be your boss's most important priority.
- Starting a habit is easier than stopping it – for example, if you constantly stay late or don't take a lunch-break it is harder to leave early or take a break another time.
- It is important to be flexible – there may be times when you will be expected to work late for a specific deadline but this does not need to become a habit.
- It is difficult to create a life outside work unless you have both the time and the energy. If you never have the opportunity or inclination to go on dates at the end of the day, you may find that a relationship deteriorates. Many divorces and separations occur because someone has not put enough into a partnership or children.

What the experts say

It is possible for individuals to create a sense of balance and harmony, even within the everyday challenges of life in the twenty-first century. It enhances self-respect and self-esteem to know what you care about, what your values are and the way you wish to live your life. Much research has been undertaken to define what work–life balance means. Robert Holden and Ben Renshaw (2002) in *Balancing Work and Life* agree with the common understanding that it means different things to different people, but they do emphasize that it is worth taking time to identify individual requirements and personal goals.

In many organizations, research has revealed that when work–life balance issues are taken into consideration people have fewer days off sick, absenteeism declines and staff morale goes up. This is clearly a financial driver to the organization, as the costs of absenteeism, staff turnover, advertising jobs, and the interviewing and training of new staff are very high. Many companies have work–life balance policies in place for everyone, and encourage people to have outside interests, because they see the benefits both for their employees and the organization as a whole. The DTI, in its 'Achieving Best Practice' project, found that: 'Employers say flexible working helps them retain skilled staff and reduce recruitment costs; raise staff morale and decrease absenteeism; and react to changing market conditions more effectively.'

Work–life balance is high on the government agenda, as there is recognition that it is having a huge impact on society and on the nation's health. In 2004, legislation was brought in stating that companies had to make allowances for parents with young children under the age of six years, permitting them to work flexi-time if the job makes it possible.

A story to share

Jane was a very successful businesswoman. She had three grown-up children, a loving husband and two beautiful houses, one in town and one in the country. It wasn't until her first grandchild was in her school Nativity play and Jane, now retired, went to watch, that she realized she had never once seen any of her three children in a play. She suddenly understood the joy of such events, the sports days and all the other occasions she had missed, that were now lost.

Three steps to understanding what work–life balance means

Each of these three exercises has been designed to encourage the students to consider what work–life balance means to them and to help them understand the importance of it in their future lives.

Exercise 17:1 Analyse your current work–life balance

This questionnaire will enable the students to find out if they currently have lives in which school and any part-time work are balanced with their leisure time.

Aim To give the students the opportunity to assess their current work–life balance.

Benefit With this quick snapshot it is possible to highlight problem areas. It also demonstrates to the students what might affect their work–life balance.

Materials required:
- Photocopies of handout 17:1 and Six Tips for each individual
- Flip chart, whiteboard or paper to record comments

Session plan
1 Introduce the idea of work–life balance, explaining its effect on people's lives.
2 Ask the students if they can think of any examples of people, either in the public eye or whom they know, who have either a good or a poor work–life balance. Encourage them to give reasons for their choices. You could prompt them with categories such as politicians, or working mothers or fathers. Write their suggestions on the left-hand side of the board or sheet of paper.
3 Then ask the students if they can think of any visible effects of either a good or a poor work–life balance (for example, tiredness and irritability or a relaxed and fulfilled attitude). Explain the more serious consequences that can result from poor work–life balance.
4 Give out the questionnaire and ask the students to complete it as honestly as possible, so that their answers reflect their typical behaviour. Point out that we often have an unusually busy time, for example leading up to exams, but what we are trying to find out is their usual way of behaving. Tell them to add up their results and then read the analysis.
5 Students might like to share what category they achieved with their friends.
6 Plenary:
- Were they surprised at the category they were put in, or is it what they expected?
- Do they agree with the comments, were they fair?
- Can they see any correlation with their results and the people listed on the board or paper?
- Do they accept that achieving a good work–life balance will be beneficial to them?
- Can they think of any times when they might be prepared to lose their work–life balance in the short term?
- Has it given them any ideas of how they might improve their work–life balance?

Work–life balance questionnaire

Circle the responses closest to your current habits at home, at school and at any part-time job:

| 1 = always | 2 = sometimes | 3 = never |

		1	2	3
1	Do you often miss homework deadlines?	1a	2b	3c
2	Are you ever late for school?	1a	2b	3c
3	Do you frequently play sport?	1c	2b	3a
4	Do you ever have trouble sleeping at night?	1a	2b	3c
5	Do you ever feel you let people down?	1a	2b	3c
6	Do you always fit in everything you want to?	1c	2b	2a
7	Do you ever feel you would like to have more time for yourself?	1a	2b	3c
8	Do you go out nearly every night of the week?	1a	2b	3c
9	Do you manage to fit your homework and coursework in?	1c	2b	3a
10	Do you ever feel stressed by your lifestyle?	1a	2b	3c

Now add up your totals   a =   , b =   , c =

Read the following analysis.

What do your answers tell us about your current work–life balance?

Mostly 'a'

From your responses, you appear to have a poor work–life balance. You should consider if you are currently living your life the way that you want to. You might find that you often put yourself under unnecessary pressure, which might have consequences for your health and your exam results and job prospects. As you get older you will probably become busier, so considering now what is important to you will help you to achieve your full potential. It might be that you have been especially busy recently and this is a temporary situation.
Take care of yourself!

Mostly 'b'

Although your current work–life balance is adequate you could probably make some improvements. There might be some areas where you could organize your time better or plan more carefully to make sure you manage to hit all of your deadlines and commitments. As you become busier, demands on your time will only increase, so making minor adjustments now could prevent you slipping into bad habits.
Take even greater care of yourself!

Mostly 'c'

Well done — you appear to have a good work–life balance and seem to be fitting lots into your life. What you will find is that you will have to continue working at it for the rest of your life, but it seems as if you are developing some good habits that will be useful to you as you get busier in the future.
Keep up the good work!

Future Directions © Diane Carrington and Helen Whitten (Network Educational Press, 2005)

Exercise 17:2 A scenario to consider. Who is the most successful and why?

This exercise requires the students to work in small groups to decide which of the individuals featured in the scenario is the most successful. Here it will become evident that there are personal differences in our definitions of success. However, it will inevitably lead to a discussion of what work–life balance issues are.

Aim To get the students to consider what success means to them, and to appreciate how some people sacrifice work–life balance to achieve material success.

Benefit An understanding of the consequences of sacrificing work–life balance in order to achieve success in terms of money and status.

Materials required:
- Photocopies of handout 17:2 and Six Tips for each individual
- Flip chart, whiteboard or paper to record learning

Session plan
1 Introduce the idea of work–life balance, explaining its effect on people's lives, or remind them of what they learned in Exercise 17:1.
2 Explain that they are going to be considering the real-life choices that people often have to make, with their careers, their families and their aspirations.
3 Ask the students to work in groups of four and give them the handout. Ask them to read the sheet in their groups and decide who is the most successful character in the story and who is the least successful.
4 Ask each group to tell you their decisions and record their answers on the board or on paper.
5 Plenary:
- Did all the groups agree on the most successful and the least successful?
- Did everyone in the group agree?
- What does this tell us about success?
- Would it make a difference if they heard that:
  - the mother had a heart attack?
  - the childminder went back to college to train to be a computer programmer?
- How could the characters in the scenario have improved their work–life balance?
- What effect would this have had on their lives and the lives of the others around them?
- Can the students learn anything from the scenario?

A story to read and consider

Sue and Ramin had been married for twelve years. They had been quite happy, with the usual ups and downs. They now had three children, who were eight, five and three years old. Sue worked as a partner in a law firm and Ramin was the director of an IT company. They both earned good money and had a beautiful six-bedroom house in the country. They had a swimming pool and a large garden for the children to play in.

Because both parents worked long hours, they had a nanny, Josie, who arrived every day at 6.00am. Sue and Ramin always caught the 6.30 train into the City of London. Both of their jobs often involved them in entertaining clients in the evening. They also often had to travel abroad, and while they were away Josie moved in with the children. If they went straight home they arrived at about 8.30pm, by which time the two youngest children were in bed, but they sometimes saw their eldest son for a little while before he, too, went to bed.

At the weekends Ramin usually played golf and Sue tried to visit her mother between taking the children to birthday parties. It was always hectic and they felt as if they were rushing around to catch up.

The days were very different for Josie. She arrived and played all day with the children. In the summer she could use the swimming pool. If Sue and Ramin were going to arrive home late, Josie's boyfriend spent the evening at the house with her, and stayed when she did. They used the large house with all its facilities as if it were their own.

Future Directions © Diane Carrington and Helen Whitten (Network Educational Press, 2005)

Exercise 17:3 Design a work–life balance poster

The students are asked to design a poster for people just starting work, explaining why work–life balance issues should be taken seriously. In selecting images and messages to be included on the poster, the students will have to decide on what they feel are the most important elements of a successful work–life balance.

Aim To give the students the opportunity to consider important elements of work–life balance for young people just starting work.

Benefit As the students will soon be in this situation, it is useful for them to think ahead about what will have an effect on their lives.

Materials required:
• Photocopy of Six Tips for each individual
• Flip chart or other paper and coloured markers, Blu-tack to display the posters
• If required, photocopies of 'What the experts say' (page 165), for ideas

Session plan
1 Introduce the idea of work–life balance, explaining its effect on people's lives, or remind the students of what they have learned from the previous two exercises.
2 Ask the students to work in groups of four or five. Explain that you want them to draw up a list of the most important elements of achieving a successful work–life balance.
3 When they have completed their lists, explain that you want them to create a poster for people just starting work to remind them of the most important elements of a successful work–life balance.
4 Display the posters on the wall and give students the opportunity to look at each other's. It might be necessary to get the groups to explain what the posters mean, if they are a little confusing!
5 Plenary:
   ■ How easy was it drawing up the list?
   ■ Did everyone in the group immediately agree?
   ■ How did they find making the posters?
   ■ What do they think of other groups' posters?
   ■ Are there many similarities?
   ■ Why might this be useful for anyone starting work to consider?
   ■ Can they learn anything from this exercise in their present position?

Achieving work–life balance

Six Tips

1 Identify your ideal balance of life and work.
2 Put your own health first: monitor your health and tiredness levels to ensure energy and stamina for important activities.
3 Discuss your needs and priorities with your boss.
4 Gain support from your work team.
5 Try to delegate tasks you are not very good at and offer to do those you are good at.
6 If you feel your values are being compromised, discuss this with your boss.

Why bother?

- When you first enter the workplace it is possible that your life outside work will not be as demanding as it might be later on, should you decide to get married or live with a partner. Therefore you can find yourself in the habit of working long hours and then when other demands occur – say, a partner or a relative becomes ill – you may find it harder to negotiate to have time off.

- Setting boundaries around what you feel is reasonable and what you are prepared to accept in the workplace can lead you to greater self-respect and this can generate respect from others.

- If you don't put yourself first and then become ill you are no good to anyone. Your good health and energy are paramount.

- If you don't consider what pressures you are letting yourself in for before you join an organization you could become disillusioned and end up leaving. Alternatively, you could adopt workaholic practices and end up becoming stressed and possibly ill. Therefore, research into the work patterns of different jobs and planning the lifestyle you desire are very important.

My first action step

Commit yourself to one action step over the next week that will help you to begin to achieve a good work–life balance.

This week I shall:

....

....

....

....

....

....

....

18 Understanding the inner self

A man's silence is wonderful to listen to.

THOMAS HARDY (1840–1928)

When you slow down, step back a moment and put things in perspective, you can then move on with more efficiency. It only takes a moment to adapt and control how you respond.

ANON

IN TODAY'S BUSY and competitive world it is sometimes difficult for young people to feel at ease doing nothing or even being alone for more than five minutes. They have been born into an era of television, videos, DVDs, gameboys and constant action, noise and attention. But a continuous external focus of attention can drain the internal and it is important to help students learn how to stop, reflect, think and just be.

The inner self, the inner life does not have to relate to any religion necessarily, although those who practise a religion are sometimes more comfortable with the concept of sitting peacefully and praying or contemplating themselves and their universe. Young people can learn to take five minutes in the middle of a busy day to stop and centre themselves, take a space, breathe and feel cool, calm and collected before continuing with the rest of their day.

This chapter gives your students the opportunity to recognize their human need for time, space, reflection, connection and imagination. It may lead to discussions of the place of religion in their lives.

The benefits of understanding the inner self

Helping your students to get to know their inner selves will be useful to them for the rest of their lives. Most people, especially young people, spend their lives rushing about and they lose sight of what is really important and what they really want to achieve. However, most of them will be aware of traditional disciplines that offer alternative solutions to the pressures of modern life. These include yoga – which is now very popular, with many fitness clubs and gyms offering sessions – and therapeutic treatments such as homeopathy and aromatherapy.

As your students have been growing up they have probably had periods when they felt under pressure and forced to act in certain ways. For example, they may have rebelled against parents and teachers because of pressure from their peers or from the media. They now need to consider how they really want to act for themselves. They need to take time to consider their personal beliefs and to decide how to live their lives for themselves. This takes quiet time, tuning in to their own thoughts and feelings. If they are true to themselves and to their personal beliefs they will feel calmer and more capable of achieving what is most important to them.

A sense of 'self' builds up over a lifetime. However, if people do not devote a reasonable amount of time to reflecting about themselves, their lives, relationships, careers and aspirations, they are likely simply to be invaded by the ideas, needs and aspirations of others. Spending time alone – a quiet evening reading, writing a diary or thinking, rather than watching television, partying and binge-drinking – can build inner strength and reinforce personal values. This helps with:

- making life decisions;
- choosing and maintaining stable relationships;
- keeping healthy (for example, maintaining low blood pressure and a normal heart rate);
- managing life events such as rejection, divorce (one's own or one's parents), bereavement, redundancy, retirement, parenting.

Considering the bigger picture gives an overview that puts life's minor struggles into perspective. Understanding their true inner selves will allow students to enjoy the journey of life and not to just focus on reaching short- or long-term goals.

What the experts say

Our brains work at different levels according to what state we are in and what we are doing. The brain operates on four main frequencies or waves: beta (13–25) cycles per second (CPS); alpha (8–12 CPS); theta (4–7 CPS); and delta (0.5–3 CPS). If you are wide awake and alert, for example, talking or trying to solve a problem at home or work, your brain is probably 'transmitting' and 'receiving' at 13 to 25 cycles per second – the beta level. However, it is when the brain is operating on the alpha wave that heightened powers of concentration and creativity are achieved. It is in this state that we are able to accomplish feats of creativity and mastery.

Daniel Goleman, in *Emotional Intelligence: Why It Can Matter More Than IQ* (1996), suggests that this state of thinking is 'emotional intelligence at its best'. All worries and fears of inadequacy are eliminated and we are able to relax and to succeed in whatever we are doing.

Another psychologist working in this field is Robert Holden, whom we mentioned in Chapter 5. He has undertaken research and has written many books on happiness, including *Happiness Now* (1998). His work has been the subject of two major TV documentaries, including QED's *How to be Happy* and the BBC's *Stress Busters*. He, too, recognizes the importance of really knowing ourselves in order to become satisfied and truly happy.

Dr Martin Seligman focuses on understanding and building the best things in life. At the individual level, this 'positive psychology' is about character strengths, including the capacity for love and work, courage, compassion, resilience, hope, creativity, social skills, integrity, self-knowledge, impulse control, future-mindedness and wisdom. In his book *Learned Optimism* (1990) Seligman explains how these attributes can be achieved by understanding our inner selves.

Recent research is proving that meditation is supportive of health, happiness and creativity. People who practise meditation are measurably healthier and have stronger immune systems than those who get addicted to 'busyness'.

Meditation does not necessarily require a person to sit for 20 minutes and chant a mantra. Taking five minutes out in the middle of a busy day to breathe slowly into the diaphragm, rather than to 'overbreathe' in the upper chest, can enhance body chemistry and allow organs to function more effectively and the brain – which takes 25 per cent of the body's oxygen reserves – to think more efficiently.

Research at the Medical College of Georgia identified that transcendental meditation reduced high blood pressure in African–American teenagers. The study tracked 156 inner-city black adolescents with elevated blood pressures. Those who practised 15 minutes of TM twice daily steadily lowered their daytime blood pressures. In addition to improving the emotional and social development of the study group, meditation eased problems of hyperactivity and loss of concentration – which inevitably has implications for study as well as brain function in general.

A story to share

Ed was someone who loved parties and company. He had grown up with several siblings and there was always noise and activity in the house. The television was usually on all the time and when he was in his bedroom he listened to his stereo; when he was travelling on public transport he would listen to his iPod. As he grew up, he found it hard to be on his own. When he started at college he would become anxious if he could not find someone to spend time with, either during the day or in the evening. He would go down to the student bar but, being essentially quite shy, did not find it easy to make new friends. If his usual circle of friends was busy doing other things he would become very stressed and end up drinking more than was good for him – which meant a hangover the next morning and falling asleep in lectures.

Eventually, his college tutor questioned Ed about his personal life and the fact that it had been reported that he sometimes fell asleep. Ed admitted to his habits and the tutor suggested that Ed set himself two nights a week to spend on his own, in his room listening to some quiet music. He also bought Ed a journal and asked him to stop and write some of his thoughts about himself and his life in the book on those evenings he spent in.

The first two nights Ed tried this it was very uncomfortable for him and he felt fidgety and strange; but over the course of three weeks he became more acclimatized to being quiet and peaceful. He found that taking this quiet time helped him to concentrate in lectures and he was also more able to express his opinion on topical subjects, as he could crystallize his thoughts more effectively.

Three steps to understanding your inner self

These exercises help students to learn to look inwards, to discover what makes them happy and to achieve a calm mind by using simple relaxation and meditation techniques.

Exercise 18:1 Moments of awe

This exercise asks the students to look back at anything they have seen, or heard or read about that gave them a sense of wonder. If they can't think of any examples, they are asked to try and imagine what the feeling might be like.

Aim To get the students to consider if they have ever experienced a moment of awe, or – if they were to in the future – what might inspire such a feeling.

Benefit It is often the smallest thing that inspires delight or enjoyment and this exercise demonstrates that we all have different triggers, which can produce a happy or inspirational feeling.

Materials required:
- Photocopies of handout 18:1 and Six Tips for each individual
- Flip chart, whiteboard or paper to record learning

Session plan
1 Introduce the idea that in getting to know our inner self it is helpful to recognize what inspires us.
2 Explain that many psychologists work in this field to help people to identify things that they enjoy. This helps us to ensure we spend time on activities that increase our happiness.
3 Ask the students to take a couple of minutes to think of something that they have seen, read about or heard that they feel was awe-inspiring, that had a 'wow' factor for them. It might be helpful to disclose a 'safe' example of your own – for example, the first snowdrop in the snow, the sound of a new-born baby crying, Man going to the Moon.
4 Give the pupils the handout and ask them to work in pairs or small groups to discuss their examples.
5 Put the following questions on the board, or call them out at the appropriate times as the discussion progresses:
   - What is your example?
   - How did it make you feel? (Ask them to try to be as detailed as possible.)
   - Are you feeling like this now, just by talking about it?
   - Do you recognize that just by talking about something you can give yourselves similar sensations of happiness and inspiration?
   - What trigger could you use to help you feel like this in the future?
6 Plenary:
   - How did the students feel doing this exercise?
   - How might they use this technique in the future to create these opportunities again?
   - Now that they have identified some factors that inspire them, how can they make sure they don't get too busy to notice them in the future?
   - In which situations would it be most helpful to focus on these moments?
   - Can they share examples of triggers that might be used?
   - How might this help them to understand their inner selves?

A sense of awe

Think back over your life and write down any moments you can recall where you felt inspired or experienced a sense of awe:

....

....

....

....

....

....

....

....

Where were you?

....

....

....

....

....

What was it about the experience that made you feel a sense of wonder?

....

....

....

....

....

....

....

Exercise 18:2 Short breathing meditation

This exercise takes the students through a simple relaxation technique that can be practised in class without any special facilities. It encourages the state of 'mindfulness', where individuals become aware that they can control the focus of their attention, removing it from outward events and drawing their minds towards a peaceful state. When they become 'mindful' they can observe themselves and choose to take control of their thinking so as to stay calm. They can practise this anywhere – even standing at a bus-stop.

Aim To enable students to understand that they have the ability to focus their minds on their breathing and achieve a calm and controlled attitude at times of stress.

Benefit This technique empowers them and gives them the ability to control their emotions and responses. Getting oxygen to the brain helps clear and creative thinking and memory processes.

Materials required:
• Flip chart, whiteboard or paper to record the learning

Session plan
1 Explain the importance of breathing deeply, which gets more oxygen into the brain and has a calming effect. Fast, shallow breathing means less oxygen is taken in and therefore less efficient brain function. Help the students to understand that they can either pay attention to what is happening outside them or can draw the focus of their attention to what is happening inside themselves. Focusing on the process of breathing can help them to do this and it can become a lifelong skill that they can practise anywhere.

2 Stand up, if possible, and lead the exercise from the front:
   ■ Ask the students to breathe in slowly through the nose for a count of 7.
   ■ Count the beats for them.
   ■ Then ask them to breathe out, blowing gently through the mouth as if blowing out a candle, for a count of 11.
   ■ Count the beats for them.

3 Explain how this has a calming effect in two ways:
   ■ The counting takes the person's mind off the problem (like counting to 10 before doing anything, when you lose your temper).
   ■ It affects you physiologically: when you expel all the carbon monoxide from your lungs it refreshes you; and more oxygen getting into the brain releases chemicals called serotonins, which act as a calming drug.

4 Plenary:
   ■ How did they feel doing the exercise?
   ■ Did they feel calmer?
   ■ How can this be used in the future?
   ■ Consider examples of different situations where this might be a useful technique.
   ■ Where might it have been useful to react in a calm, controlled manner in the past?

Exercise 18:3 Mind and body relaxation

This is a longer relaxation exercise to refresh the whole body. It requires space for the students to sit quietly as you lead them through the relaxation sheet.

Aim To introduce the technique of relaxing mind and body whenever the student requires some calm and peace.

Benefit This technique has proven health benefits.

Materials required:
• Photocopies of handout 18:3 and Six Tips for each individual
• A chair for each individual

Session plan
1 Introduce the concept of meditation. Discuss and share what they already know about this – for example, transcendental meditation, yoga, t'ai chi and martial arts. Explain that many sportspeople learn to focus their minds in order to achieve success.
2 Explain that you are going to introduce them to a short relaxation technique that they can practise for themselves whenever they feel stressed or whenever they feel they would benefit from developing a calm state.
3 Ask the students to put down pens and paper and relax. Tell them that this is not a time to worry about whether other people are watching them, but ten minutes in which they can really focus on themselves and take a quiet moment to stop thinking.
4 Read the relaxation sheet slowly and give them some time to sit in silence and visualize.
5 After they have refocused, suggest they stand up and stretch in order to feel refreshed.
6 Plenary:
   ■ How did this feel?
   ■ Have they experienced a relaxation meditation before?
   ■ Do they feel calmer?
   ■ [If appropriate] Were they able to experience a feeling of being loved and valued exactly as they are, for their inner selves?
   ■ Would this technique help them when they are stressed?
   ■ Can they think about how they might adapt this technique and practise meditating in their daily lives, even if only for three to five minutes from time to time?

Relaxation meditation sheet for the session leader

Ask the students to put down pen and paper and to sit comfortably in their chairs. Explain that this is not a time to worry about feeling shy or embarrassed but a time when they can stop and focus on themselves and relax. Ask them to give their commitment to enabling the success of the exercise for the whole group, as one person fidgeting can distract other people. Make sure they have their mobile phones switched off. When they are ready and prepared, read the following to them slowly and calmly:

'Now that you are sitting relaxing in your chairs you can start to take your thinking away from observing the outside world and shift the focus of your attention into your own minds. When you are ready, you can close your eyes and breathe normally and easily.

Take your attention to your forehead. Just focus your attention on your forehead… relax any tension you notice there and keep your mental attention on the area between your eyebrows…you may notice a slight tingling there as you focus.

Now take your attention to your eyes. Soften the area around your eyes. Release any tension you may have built up in this area and rest your eyes. Gradually drop your attention to your jaw and relax your jaw and the muscles around the jaw, as these take in stress and tension during the day.

In a minute I am going to ask you to take a deep breath in, hold it for the count of 3 and then slowly release the breath over the count of 6.

So…take a deep breath in – feel it go into your diaphragm at the lower end of your ribs. Hold it for the count of 1 – 2 – 3 and then slowly breathe out 1 – 2 – 3 – 4 – 5 – 6. Then take another deep breath in and hold it to the count of 3. This time as you breathe out, allow your neck and shoulders to relax and then breathe normally and easily in your own rhythm.

Gradually take your attention to your arms, hands, fingers and allow each area to relax. Feel the tension slip away. Notice your spine, your legs, ankles, feet, toes and allow each area of your body to relax. Notice your breath going in…and out…in…and out…

Then focus your mind on a beautiful scene – a green pasture of spring flowers. Find yourself seated there and notice the greens of the grass and imagine the different colours of the flowers. Imagine butterflies of brilliant colours drifting peacefully in the sunshine. Hear the sound of the birds in the trees. Imagine yourself inside this scene and notice how you can feel relaxed here, away from the pressures of life, a quiet still place in your mind that you can go to any time you choose.

I shall leave you in this peaceful place, in silence, for just one minute so that your mind can get used to being still, to experiencing silence. I shall lead you out of the relaxation at the end of this minute.'

[If you think it would be beneficial to the students, you could ask a question before you leave them in silence – such as, 'Imagine the world loves and values you exactly the way you are: what would that feel like?' Then, if appropriate, leave them in silence for one minute – or longer if you feel this would be helpful.]

'Now you can start to take yourself away from the pasture or wherever your mind has taken you and start to become aware of your body in this room. Take your attention down to your feet and toes and begin to feel the energy returning to them and revitalizing them. Draw your attention up to your spine and feel the energy revitalizing your spine so that it is strong and refreshed.

Notice your breathing and imagine taking in a deep breath of energy and letting go, on the out-breath, of any sleepiness so that you are beginning to feel refreshed and alive.

Finally, take your attention to your neck, shoulders and head and feel the energy returning to these areas so that as you open your eyes you feel refreshed and alive and ready to face the rest of the day with energy.

As you open your eyes take a stretch…'

Meditation

Take some quiet time alone or with a close friend. Repeat the meditation exercise you did with the teacher. This can refresh both mind and body.

Sit quietly for a moment and take some slow deep breaths. You do not have to make an 'effort' to breathe, just keep it gentle.

Begin to relax your mind and take the focus of your attention inside yourself.

Follow the process that your teacher showed you:

1 Close your eyes and take a deep breath, hold it for the count of 3 and then release it for the count of 6.

2 Repeat this deep breath once more and then start to breathe normally in your own rhythm.

3 With each breath, gradually start to relax every part of your body. Allow the 'chatter' of your mind to quieten so that you are just focusing on your breathing. Take the focus of your mind down your body and relax each part in turn, visualizing all of your body as healthy and perfect. Start from your forehead and brain, down to your eyes, neck, shoulders, jaw, back, down your legs to your feet. This can take as short or as long a time as you want.

4 When you are ready, you can bring your attention up from your feet towards your head. As your focus goes through each part of your body, visualize it refreshed and healthy and re-energized to manage the rest of your day.

5 When you reach your head again, open your eyes and stretch.

Future Directions © Diane Carrington and Helen Whitten (Network Educational Press, 2005)

Understanding your inner self

Six Tips

1 Take a few minutes as you get ready for work in the morning to increase your awareness and observation – for example, notice the colours in your bedroom.

2 On your way to school stop and focus your mind on your breathing – notice the in-breath and the out-breath. Allow this focus to help you to feel calm and peaceful wherever you are.

3 Notice the pattern of your thoughts on a daily basis – what sort of things are you thinking about? Do these thoughts reflect who you are and the sort of things you personally care about?

4 Take two evenings a week when you stay in, turn off the TV and just stop and listen to music and reflect on how you are managing your life.

5 Keep a journal and capture your inner thoughts – the things you care about; your goals and values; your ideas about life. This helps you to develop your 'sense of self'.

6 Practise the relaxation meditation once or twice a day. Even three to five minutes mental focus and relaxation can improve your ability to concentrate and to listen well.

Why bother?

■ We live in a world where people tend to have an 'external' focus and we neglect the 'inner' life of thought and emotions. The external is tempting and provides endless distraction and activity. The internal focus can be difficult to master at first but the more you take some time alone to stop and get control of your thoughts, breathing and emotions the more you will find that you are able to focus and concentrate in other places.

■ Mental focus has been proven to enhance concentration and performance before exams or sports events.

■ Relaxation and meditation has been proven to increase longevity and enhance health and well-being.

■ Taking time to work out who you are and what your own thoughts about a situation are enables you to express your opinions more articulately. This ensures that they really are your own thoughts and not someone else's because you haven't bothered to take the time to consider your own opinions.

My first action step

Commit yourself to one action step over the next week that will help you to develop understanding of your inner self.

This week I shall:

....

....

....

....

19 Continuous development

Life is like playing a violin in public and learning the instrument as one goes on.
SAMUEL BUTLER (1835–1902)

A journey of 10,000 miles starts with a single step.
CHINESE PROVERB

THE THEORIES, models and activities that have been included in this book represent a starting point for a lifetime's journey of self-awareness and self-management. Often, young people leaving school imagine that they may never have to study or learn again. They may believe that adults know most things by the time they reach their mid-twenties, and may not realize that people continue to learn new things and ways of behaving until the day they die. This chapter aims to help the students realize that they will benefit from continuing to build on their skills and to reinforce their learning day by day for the rest of their lives.

The benefits of continuous development

Retaining a sense of self-observation and self-analysis can help people to learn from events and enhance their relationships, their work performance and their ability to be happy and manage different situations. Students are likely to change their careers many times in their working lives and will need to adapt and learn new information and skills. The art of continuous review of goals, values, behaviour and communication styles enables a person to develop emotional maturity and enhance his or her ability to manage the world of work.

What the experts say

Stephen Covey, who wrote *The Seven Habits of Highly Effective People* (1989), explains that to 'sharpen the saw' is an essential part of being effective. This means that people should always value what they do know but, equally, consider and identify what they do not yet know. 'Sharpening the saw' is to raise the bar, and to seek new skills, information and challenges in order to stay capable of meeting new situations throughout life.

Tony Buzan advises people to 'make the most of their mind' by continuing to learn new skills and information. Buzan and other specialists in thinking skills argue that if you do not use your brain you lose it – memory and cognitive faculties improve with use.

Most people have times when they study, or use their brains in a more intensive way than they do at other times of their life. The good thing is that neuroscientists are

Future Directions   **19** Continuous development

proving that we can re-activate our brains at any stage. We now witness this by the fact that many people who did not get a degree earlier in life are taking degrees in their 70s or 80s and proving that their brains were always perfectly capable of such achievement.

A story to share

David had not achieved good qualifications at school. He took a job as a gardener for a local authority. He worked hard and earned a small salary but he managed his budget satisfactorily.

After a few years he became frustrated that he had not studied harder at school. At the age of 32 he decided to go to teachers' training college, where he studied hard and qualified. He felt delighted that he had managed this challenge, which took more than just academic study as he had to learn new behaviours in order to be able to manage himself, his time and his ability to manage a class of children.

Eventually David became headteacher at one of the major secondary schools in the north of England.

Three steps to continuous development

These three exercises help students consider what the future might look like and how they can build on the skills, knowledge and information they have gained from the lessons in this book.

Exercise 19:1 Learning review

This exercise helps students to reflect on the lessons and exercises they have undertaken so far, and to consider what will be most useful to them in the future.

Aim To consolidate all that the students have learned and to help them to identify which aspects of the programme have been most useful and will support their continuing journey.

Benefit This review exercise gives shape to the skills and knowledge that the students have learned and the insights they may have had, so that they can continue to build on them.

Materials required:
• Photocopies of handout 19:1 and Six Tips for each individual
• Flip chart, whiteboard or paper to record feedback

Session plan
1 Explain that the skills, knowledge and exercises they have undertaken during the programme represent a first step in a lifetime's journey of learning.
2 Give them the handout and explain that this is an opportunity to reflect and consider which exercises were most helpful and interesting to them.
3 Ask them to consider how they can build on their learning and use it to help them in their adult lives.
4 Give them ten minutes in groups of three to write down their thoughts.
5 Plenary:
   ■ What has been most useful?
   ■ Did anyone have some real insights into what might help him or her in the future?
   ■ How can they build on these skills and information?

Learning review

What did you find most useful about the exercises you undertook in this programme?

....

....

What insights did you get into your own behaviour?

....

....

What insights did you get into other people's behaviour?

....

....

What insights did you get into life?

....

....

What skill-sets do you feel you have acquired?

....

....

In what ways have you come to understand better the challenges you will experience in the adult world?

....

....

How can you use your knowledge and skills to help you on the continuing journey through your life?

....

....

Future Directions © Diane Carrington and Helen Whitten (Network Educational Press, 2005)

Exercise 19:2 Learning possibilities

This exercise asks students to use some creativity and write a 'rap' poem about future learning.

Aim To help students identify what situations they may face in the future where they will need to learn new skills, knowledge and behaviours.

Benefit Helps students understand that they must remain flexible and ready to adapt to new challenges, and that the programme they have just undertaken will help them do so successfully.

Materials required:
- Photocopies of handout 19:2 and Six Tips for each individual
- Flip chart or paper to record any feedback

Session plan
1 Explain that the students will face many new situations throughout their lives where they will need to continue to learn new information, skills and ways of behaving.
2 Put them in groups of six. Ask them to think about different situations they may encounter – for example, leaving school, leaving home, starting work, getting married, having children, changing job, getting promoted.
3 Ask them to write a 'rap' poem that includes some of these situations and identifies some of the new skills or information they may need to learn. This is designed to be a fun exercise, so help them to feel at ease with the prospect of creating the poem.
4 Give them 20 minutes to brainstorm the situation and write the 'rap' poem.
5 Ask each group to read the poem to the class.
6 Plenary:
   - Was it easy to consider situations where they may need to learn new skills and information?
   - Were there more or fewer situations than they had imagined when they started the exercise?
   - Can they give examples of people they know or have seen adapting to these kind of situations?
   - What behaviours and emotions are most helpful to them in managing new challenges?

The learning possibilities rap

This exercise is designed to help you identify situations you may face in the future where you will need to learn new:

skills
knowledge
information
behaviours.

Please record some of these situations in the space below:

....

....

....

....

....

Now create, as a group, a 'rap' poem that identifies some of these situations and also some of the new skills, behaviours and knowledge you may need to acquire in order to manage the situations effectively:

Exercise 19:3 Change success

The shift from education to the workplace is a transition period and the students will continue to experience many other transitions in their lifetimes. This exercise helps them to consider what they might like to 'cast off' from the 'old me' that may no longer be appropriate to a new life. They will also consider what the 'new me' might look like.

Aim To help students understand the process of change and to be prepared to manage transitional periods throughout their lives.

Benefit Reminds them how the brain builds habits of thought and behaviour and how they can change these patterns to be who they need to be in the next phase of life.

Materials required:
- Photocopies of handout 19:3 (see *www.networkpress.co.uk/resources* for colour version) and Six Tips for each individual
- Plain paper and coloured pens for drawing
- Flip chart, whiteboard or paper

Session plan
1 Give the students the handout and remind them how the brain develops habits of thought and behaviour through repetition (as explained in Chapter 3). Use the handout to explain how the consciousness and learning process works. You might need to enlarge this on the board, or on paper, to make sure the students understand.
2 Explain that the brain can be trained to develop new pathways and that when people face a change of situation they need to change old habits and develop new and more constructive ones.
3 Give the students a piece of paper each and ask them to draw a picture of themselves as 'The Old Me'. This picture should symbolically represent them with their old habits, body language, friends and environment.
4 Get them to share this and start to consider what habits may be inappropriate in their new adult life of college or work. List these by whatever means appropriate.
5 Now get the students each to take a new piece of paper and draw 'The New Me'. This picture should symbolically represent the new habits they feel will help them to manage adult life.
6 Plenary:
   - What new habits will help them succeed in the adult world?
   - What old habits will hinder their success?
   - How can they start to develop the new neural pathways of thought and behaviour to achieve this change? (You could remind them of Exercise 5:1, in which they learned that changing thoughts can impact emotions.)
   - How can they support one another on this continuous journey?
   - What is one word that will remind them to feel confident as they move towards the future?

Change success

Your brain's learning mechanism is designed to develop habits of thought and behaviour so as to release the conscious mind to focus on new information, or concentrate on specific situations. The diagram below demonstrates four steps to learning: (1) not even knowing the topic exists; (2) trying to do it but not succeeding; (3) becoming adept but having to focus; and (4) being able to do it without thinking. Each subject or task you learn follows a similar pathway. This four-step process relates to your learning skills, information and also new behaviours.

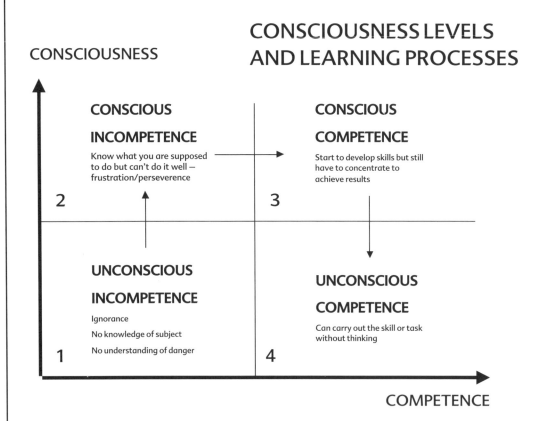

CONSCIOUSNESS

CONSCIOUSNESS LEVELS AND LEARNING PROCESSES

CONSCIOUS INCOMPETENCE
Know what you are supposed to do but can't do it well — frustration/perseverence

2

CONSCIOUS COMPETENCE
Start to develop skills but still have to concentrate to achieve results

3

UNCONSCIOUS INCOMPETENCE
Ignorance
No knowledge of subject
No understanding of danger

1

UNCONSCIOUS COMPETENCE
Can carry out the skill or task without thinking

4

COMPETENCE

Draw two pictures

Now take a sheet of paper and draw:
1 'The Old Me': a picture symbolizing yourself with your old habits.

2 'The New Me: a picture symbolizing yourself with new habits that will help you manage college and work.

Continuous development

Six Tips

1 Choose a study subject or career that excites you and plays to your strengths.

2 Give your brain a stretch into new areas.

3 Allow your brain to imagine and play – it aids learning and creativity.

4 Repeat and practise the new habits so that they become 'unconscious competence'.

5 Be the person you want to see and create the world you want to be living in.

6 Recognize your success and continue to dream.

Why bother?

- You need to make the most of each day, to be marketable and to ensure that you are contributing your best for yourself and your employer.

- There are many opportunities available to you and feeling confident in your ability to learn, adapt and change to meet these situations is a key to your success.

My first action step

Commit yourself to one action in the next week that will help you to learn well and build new habits to support your continuous development.

This week I shall:

....

....

....

....

....

....

Good Luck and Start Living Your Dreams Now!

Future Directions © Diane Carrington and Helen Whitten (Network Educational Press, 2005)

References

Basadur, M.S. (1995), *The Power of Innovation*, Pitman Professional Publishing

Bennis, Warren and Biederman, Patricia Ward (1997), *Organising Genius*, Nicholas Brealey Publishing

Berne, Eric (1964), *Games People Play*, Penguin Books

Berne, Eric (1990), *What do you say after you say Hello?*, Corgi Books

Buzan, Tony (2002), *How to Mind Map*, Thorsons

Buzan, Tony and Barry (2003), *The Mind Map Book*, BBC Books

Cameron, Julia (1995), *The Artist's Way*, Pan

Career 2000, The Guardian

Carter, Rita (1999), *Mapping the Mind*, Seven Dials

Covey, Stephen R. (1989), *The Seven Habits of Highly Effective People*, Simon & Schuster

De Bono, Edward (1990), *Six Thinking Hats*, Penguin Books

Dryden, Windy (1993), *Peak Performance*, Mercury

Fletcher, Winston (2002), *Beating the 24/7: How Business Leaders Achieve a Successful Work–Life Balance*, John Wiley & Sons

Gardner, Howard (1993), *Creating Minds*, BasicBooks

Gawain, Shakti (1978), *Creative Visualisation*, New World Library

Greenfield, Susan (1996), *The Human Mind Explained*, Cassell

Greenfield, Susan (2000), *Brain Story*, BBC

Greenfield, Susan (2000), *The Private Life of the Brain*, Allen Lane

Goleman, Daniel (1996), *Emotional Intelligence*, Bloomsbury Publishing

Hall, Alvin (2003), *Your Money or Your Life: A Practical Guide to Solving Your Financial Problems and Affording a Life You'll Love*, Hodder & Stoughton

Handy, Charles (1997), *The Hungry Spirit*, Hutchinson

Herrmann, Ned (1996), *The Whole Brain Business Book*, McGraw-Hill

Holden, Robert (1993), *Laughter, the Best Medicine*, Thorsons

Holden, Robert (1998), *Happiness Now*, Hodder & Stoughton

Holden, Robert and Renshaw, Ben (2002), *Balancing Work and Life*, Dorling Kindersley

Howard, Pierce J. (2000), *The Owner's Manual for the Brain*, 2nd edn, Bard Press

Israel, I., Whitten, H. and Shaffran, C. (2000), *Your Mind at Work*, Kogan Page

James, Jennifer (1997), *Thinking in the Future Tense*, Touchstone Books, New York

James, Muriel and Jongeward, Dorothy (1996), *Born to Win*, Perseus Books

Jeffers, Susan (1991), *Feel the Fear and Do it Anyway*, Arrow Books

Lundin, Stephen (2000), *Fish*, Hodder & Stoughton

McDaniels, Carl (1990), *The Changing Workplace: Career Counselling Strategies for the 1990s and Beyond*, Josey-Bass

Moir, Anne and Jessel, David (1992), *Brainsex*, Mandarin

Mukerjea, Dilip (1998), *Braindancing*, The Brainware Press

O'Brien, Dominic (1993), *How to Develop a Perfect Memory*, Pavilion Books

O'Connor, Joseph and Seymour, John (1990), *Introducing Neuro-linguistic Programming*, Mandala

Palmer, Stephen and Strickland, Lynda (1996), *Stress Management: A Quick Guide*, Folens

Pert, Candida (1998), *Molecules of Emotion*, Simon & Schuster

Pinker, Steven (1997), *How the Mind Works*, W.W. Norton, New York

Pinker, Steven (2002), *The Blank Slate*, Penguin Books

Prashnig, Barbara (1998), *The Power of Diversity*, Network Educational Press

Richardson, Robert J. and Thayer, S. Katharine (1993), *The Charisma Factor*, Prentice Hall

Ridley, Matt (1993), *The Red Queen*, Penguin Books

Rose, Colin (1987), *Accelerated Learning*, Dell

Russell, Peter (1979), *The Brain Book*, Routledge & Kegan Paul

Savickas, Mark L. and Walsh, W. Bruce (1996), *Handbook of Career Counselling Theory and Practice*, David Black Publishing

Seligman, Martin Dr. (1990), *Learned Optimism*, Pocket Books

Siler, Todd (1997), *Think Like a Genius*, Bantam, New York

Smith, Alistair (2002), *The Brain's Behind It*, Network Educational Press

Snyder, C.R. and Lopez, Shane J. (eds) (2002), *Handbook of Positive Psychology*, Oxford University Press

The Times (2004), *A-Z of Careers and Jobs*, Kogan Page

Whitten, Helen, Israel, Richard and Shaffran, Cliff (2000), *Your Mind at Work*, Kogan Page

Winston, Robert (2003), *The Human Mind*, Bantam Press

Wise, Anna (1997), *The High Performance Mind*, Jeremy P. Tarcher, New Yor

Resources

Diane Carrington and Helen Whitten offer coaching and training on positive life strategies for young people, including study skills and training for teachers. They can be contacted at:

www.positiveworks.com
Tel: 020 7736 1417
Email:info@positiveworks.com

The following list provides contact details for other supportive organizations and sources of useful advice. You may wish to display this information in the classroom.

General
www.agetalks.com
Consultancy on age inclusion and age discrimination

www.connexions.gov.uk
Confidential advice, support and information for young people

www.stephencovey.com
(See chapter 15)

www.davidco.com
David Allen's site (see chapter 15)

www.hbdi-uk.com
Information on the Herrmann Brain Dominance Instrument

www.info4yp.demon.co.uk/HOUSING.HTM
Information on housing

www.mind-map.com/EN/
Details of Tony Buzan's training courses

www.networkpress.co.uk

www.parentlineplus.org.uk

www.youth2youth.co.uk/
Or telephone the Helpline: 020 8896 3675
General youth concerns

Careers
www.givemeajob.co.uk

www.icg-uk.org
Career guidance

www.jobsunlimited.co.uk

Crisis
www.bullying.co.uk

www.childline.org.uk/helpandadvice.asp
Or telephone the Helpline: 0800 1111

Samaritans: email **jo@samaritans.org**; or telephone 08457 90 90 90

Drugs
www.talktofrank.com/

Health
www.bbc.co.uk/radio1/onelife/health

www.channel4.com/health/stress

www.lifebytes.gov.uk/indexmenu.html
Emotional health and well-being

www.mindbodysoul.gov.uk/

www.rethink.org/at-ease/siteindex.htm
Advice on stress

Sex
www.playingsafely.co.uk/

Network Educational Press – much more than publishing...

NEP Conferences – Invigorate your teaching

Each term NEP runs a wide range of conferences on cutting edge issues in teaching and learning at venues around the UK. The emphasis is always highly practical. Regular presenters include some of our top-selling authors such as Sue Palmer, Mike Hughes and Steve Bowkett. Dates and venues for our current programme of conferences can be found on our website www.networkpress.co.uk.

NEP online Learning Style Analysis – Find out how your students prefer to learn

Discovering what makes your students tick is the key to personalizing learning. NEP's Learning Style Analysis is a 50-question online evaluation that can give an immediate and thorough learning profile for every student in your class. It reveals how, when and where they learn best, whether they are right brain or left brain dominant, analytic or holistic, whether they are strongly auditory, visual, kinesthetic or tactile ... and a great deal more. And for teachers who'd like to take the next step, LSA enables you to create a whole-class profile for precision lesson planning.

Developed by The Creative Learning Company in New Zealand and based on the work of Learning Styles expert Barbara Prashnig, this powerful tool allows you to analyse your own and your students' learning preferences in a more detailed way than any other product we have ever seen. To find out more about Learning Style Analysis or to order profiles visit www.networkpress.co.uk/lsa.

Also available: *Teaching Style Analysis* and *Working Style Analysis*.

NEP's Critical Skills Programme – Teach your students skills for lifelong learning

The Critical Skills Programme puts pupils at the heart of learning, by providing the skills required to be successful in school and life. Classrooms are developed into effective learning environments, where pupils work collaboratively and feel safe enough to take 'learning risks'. Pupils have more ownership of their learning across the whole curriculum and are encouraged to develop not only subject knowledge but the fundamental skills of:

- problem solving
- creative thinking
- decision making
- communication
- management
- organization

- leadership
- self-direction
- quality working
- collaboration
- enterprise
- community involvement

'The Critical Skills Programme... energizes students to think in an enterprising way. CSP gets students to think for themselves, solve problems in teams, think outside the box, to work in a structured manner. CSP is the ideal way to forge an enterprising student culture.'

Rick Lee, Deputy Director, Barrow Community Learning Partnership

To find out more about CSP training visit the Critical Skills Programme website at
www.criticalskills.co.uk